HANDY REFERENCE - Keyboard

Ctrl+O ....Opens
Ctrl+S .... Saves the active database component
Ctrl+P .... Prints the active database
Ctrl+Z or Alt+Backspace .... Undoes the last action

Ctrl+C ....Copies selection to Windows Clipboard
Ctrl+X ....Deletes selection and places copy in Clipboard
Ctrl+V or Shift+Insert.. Pastes in Clipboard contents

Ctrl+F .... Carries out a Find operation
Ctrl+H .... Carries out a Find-and-Replace operation

Ctrl+:..Inserts current time
Ctrl+;..Inserts current date
Ctrl+Alt+Spacebar................. Inserts default value for a field (if applicable)
Ctrl+' .... Inserts the value from the same field in the previous record
Ctrl++ .... Inserts a new blank record
Ctrl+- ....Deletes the active record

In datasheets

F2 .... Switches between Edit and Navigation modes
Tab ....Moves to next field
Shift+Tab .... Moves to previous field
End .... Moves to last field in active record
Home .... Moves to first field in active record
Down cursor .... Moves to the active field in the next record
Up cursor .... Moves to the active field in the previous record
Ctrl+End.. Moves to the last field in the last record
Ctrl+Home .... Moves to the first field in the first record

Ctrl+W .... Closes the active database
Alt+F4...Closes Access

ABOUT THE SERIES

In easy steps series is developed for time-sensitive people who want results fast. It is designed for quick, easy and effortless learning.

By using the best authors in the field, and with our experience in writing computer training materials, this series is ideal for today's computer users. It explains the essentials simply, concisely and clearly - without the unnecessary verbal blurb. We strive to ensure that each book is technically superior, effective for easy learning and offers the best value.

Learn the essentials **in easy steps** - accept no substitutes!

Titles in the series include:

Title	Author	ISBN
Windows 95	Harshad Kotecha	1-874029-28-8
Microsoft Office	Stephen Copestake	1-874029-37-7
Internet UK	Andy Holyer	1-874029-31-8
CompuServe UK	John Clare	1-874029-33-4
CorelDRAW	Stephen Copestake	1-874029-32-6
PageMaker	Scott Basham	1-874029-35-0
Quicken UK	John Sumner	1-874029-30-X
Microsoft Works	Stephen Copestake	1-874029-41-5
Word	Scott Basham	1-874029-39-3
Excel	Pamela Roach	1-874029-40-7
Sage Sterling for Windows	Ralf Kirchmayr	1-874029-43-1
Sage Instant Accounting	Ralf Kirchmayr	1-874029-44-X
SmartSuite	Stephen Copestake	1-874029-42-3
HTML	Ralf Kirchmayr	1-874029-46-6
Netscape Navigator	Mary Lojkine	1-874029-47-4
PagePlus	Richard Hunt	1-874029-49-0
Publisher	Brian Austin	1-874029-56-3
Access	Stephen Copestake	1-874029-57-1
Internet Explorer	Mary Lojkine	1-874029-58-X
WordPerfect	Stephen Copestake	1-874029-59-8

To order or for details on forthcoming titles ask your bookseller or contact Computer Step on 01926 817999.

ACCESS
in easy steps

Stephen Copestake

In easy steps is an imprint of Computer Step
5c Southfield Road, Southam
Warwickshire CV33 OJH England
☎01926 817999

First published 1996
Copyright © 1996 by Computer Step

Notice of Liability
Every effort has been made to ensure that this book contains accurate
and current information. However, Computer Step and the author
shall not be liable for any loss or damage suffered by readers as a
result of any information contained herein.

Trademarks
Microsoft and Windows are registered trademarks of Microsoft
Corporation. All other trademarks are acknowledged as belonging to
their respective companies.

For all sales and volume discounts please contact Computer Step on
Tel: 01926 817999.

For export orders and reprint/translation rights write to the address
above or Fax: (+44) 1926 817005.

Printed and bound in the United Kingdom

ISBN 1-874029-57-1

Contents

First steps

CHAPTER ONE

This chapter gives you the fundamentals of starting Access for the first time. It provides brief details of ways in which you can customise some of its basic features to your own requirements. You'll learn how to add new buttons to toolbars, and how to specify which toolbars display. You'll also learn to use Access' on-line Help system, including the Answer Wizard, a new way of interacting with Help which lets you frame questions in the way *you* want. Finally, you'll learn how to close down Access.

Covers

Starting Access (1)

You can launch Access in a variety of ways. If you bought Access as part of the Microsoft Office Professional suite, the following method is perhaps the easiest to use.

Running Access

Press Ctrl+Esc. Now do the following:

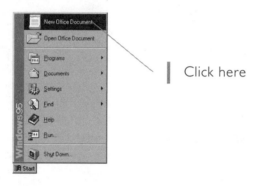

| Click here

Access lets you create a blank database, as here, when you launch it, or a database based on a specific template or wizard. (See Chapter 2 for how to use templates and wizards.)

2 Click this tab

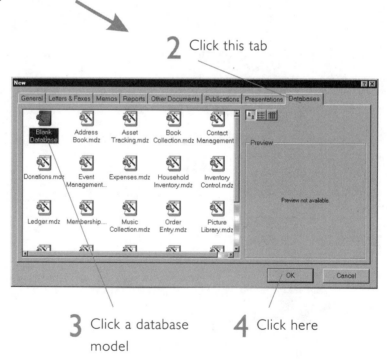

3 Click a database model

4 Click here

Starting Access (2)

Here, we're concerned with launching Access with a blank database. Now do the following:

Click here

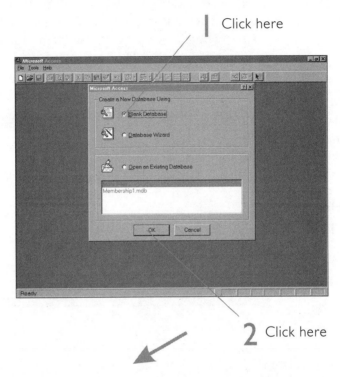

2 Click here

3 Click here; select the drive/folder you want to host the new database

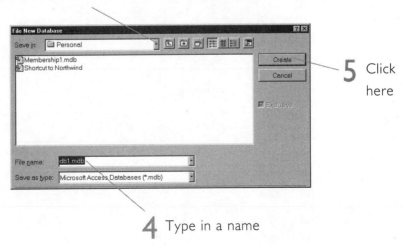

5 Click here

4 Type in a name

Starting Access (3)

There are two further dialogs which have to be negotiated. After step 2 below, Access launches a straightforward database in Datasheet view (this is a way of viewing database data which is strongly reminiscent of spreadsheets – see Chapter 5 for more information).

REMEMBER **This process creates a very simple database. For how to create a more complex one, see Chapter 2.**

Click here

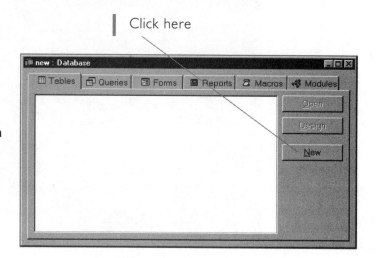

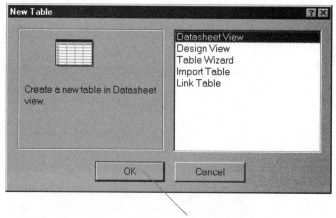

2 Click here

The Access screen

Below is a detailed illustration of a typical Access screen:

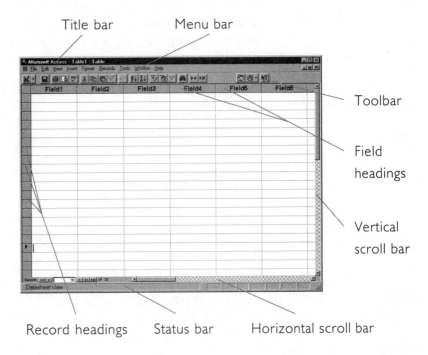

Title bar

Menu bar

Toolbar

Field headings

Vertical scroll bar

Record headings   Status bar   Horizontal scroll bar

Some of these – e.g. the rulers and scroll bars – are standard to just about all programs which run under Windows 95. One – the Status bar – can be hidden, if required.

Specifying whether the Status bar displays

Pull down the Tools menu and click Options. Then do the following:

You can also hide or show specific toolbars; see the 'Toolbars (1)' topic next.

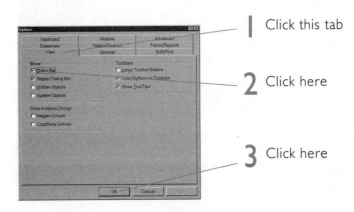

1 Click this tab

2 Click here

3 Click here

Toolbars (1)

Toolbars are important components in Access. A toolbar is an on-screen bar which contains shortcut buttons. These symbolise and allow easy access to often-used commands which would normally have to be invoked via one or more menus.

For example, Access' Table Datasheet toolbar lets you:

• save and print documents

• perform copy-and-paste and cut-and-paste operations

• launch Print Preview

• switch to different views

• launch Access' HELP system

by simply clicking on the relevant button.

Access provides 19 separate toolbars. We'll be looking at several of these in more detail as we encounter them. For the moment, some general advice.

Specifying which toolbars are displayed

Pull down the View menu and click on Toolbars. Now do the following:

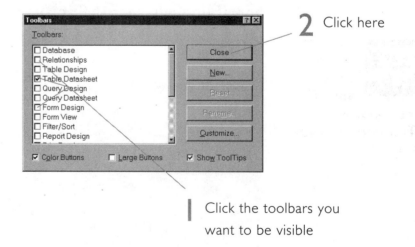

2 Click here

Click the toolbars you want to be visible

Toolbars (2)

Adding buttons to toolbars

By default, the pre-defined toolbars which come with Access have only a comparatively small number of buttons associated with them (for instance, the Table Datasheet toolbar has 21, while the Database toolbar – which you'll probably use frequently – has 23). However, just about all editing operations you can perform from within Access menus can be incorporated (for ease of access) as a button within the toolbar of your choice. The process is convenient and easy to implement.

First make sure the toolbar you want to add one or more buttons to is visible (see the 'Toolbars (1)' topic for how to do this). Move the mouse pointer over the toolbar and right-click once. In the menu which appears, click Customize. Now do the following:

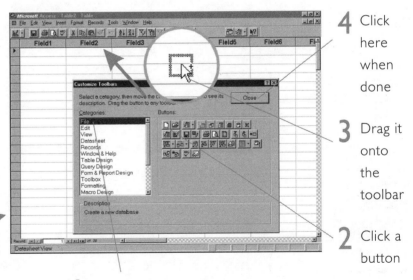

4 Click here when done

3 Drag it onto the toolbar

2 Click a button

Click the menu you want to add a button to

If in doubt, move the mouse pointer over any button in the dialog; Access tells you what it does in the Description field.

Toolbars (3)

You can also remove buttons from toolbars, and adjust the intervals between buttons.

Deleting toolbar buttons

First make sure the relevant toolbar is visible (see the 'Toolbars (1)' topic for how to do this). Move the mouse pointer over the toolbar and right-click once. In the menu which appears, click Customize. Now do the following:

Click a button

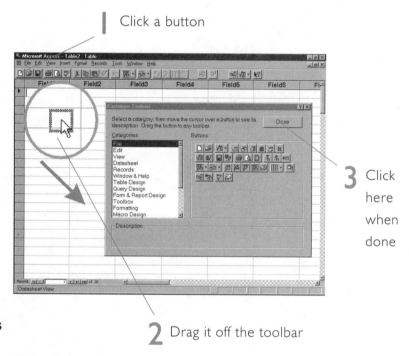

3 Click here when done

The arrows in the After image indicate the inserted space, and are purely for illustration purposes.

2 Drag it off the toolbar

Adjusting button spacing

First, launch the Customize Toolbars dialog (see above). To insert a space between two buttons, drag one of them to the right or left *by almost half the width of the button.*

Before...   After

Finally, follow step 3 above.

Using the Access Help system (1)

Access has comprehensive Help facilities, organised under two broad headings:

• Contents (a nested list of topics)

• Index (an alphabetical list of topics)

To generate either of these, pull down the Help menu and choose Microsoft Access Help Topics.

Using Contents

Carry out step 1 to begin searching for the topic you need, or step 2 to cancel your search.

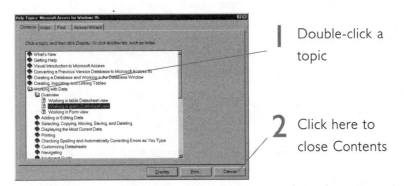

1 Double-click a topic

2 Click here to close Contents

After step 1, Access launches a series of subheadings. When you find the topic you want information on (prefixed by 🄿), double-click on it.

REMEMBER

Re step 2 – sometimes, Access launches a further dialog now:

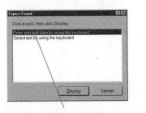

Double-click a sub-topic for assistance.

Using Index

Carry out steps 1-2 below (or 3 to close Help):

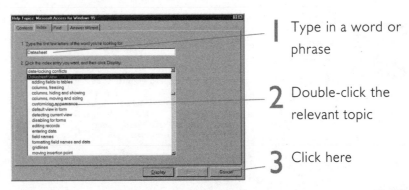

1 Type in a word or phrase

2 Double-click the relevant topic

3 Click here

Using the Access Help system (2)

When you've used the Contents or Index sections of Help to pick the topic you want help with, Access displays it as a separate window. Carry out steps 1-3 below, as appropriate:

Re step 2 – here, the Back button is greyed out - and therefore unavailable - because no Help topics were previously referred to in this session.

Click here to return to Index or Contents

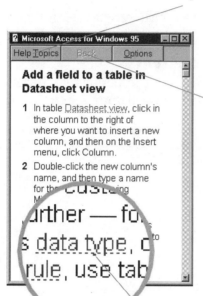

2 Click here to return to an earlier topic (if applicable)

This is a magnified view of a link - see step 3.

3 Click any link (underlined) to launch a special explanatory Help box:

Press Esc at any time to close down a Help window or box.

data type

The attribute of a variable or field that determines what kind of data it can hold. For example, the Text and Memo field data types allow the field to store either text or numbers, but the Number data type will allow only numbers to be stored in the field. Supported data types include field data types, Visual Basic data types, and query parameter data types.

Using the Access Help system (3)

Other Help features Access supports include the following:

Access calls these highly specific Help bubbles 'ToolTips'. ToolTips are a specialised form of ScreenTips (see below).

- moving the mouse pointer over toolbar buttons produces an explanatory Help bubble:

- moving the mouse pointer over fields in dialogs, commands or screen areas and right-clicking produces a specific Help box. Carry out the following procedure to activate this.

Access calls these highly specific Help topics 'ScreenTips'.

Left-click here for the specific Help topic

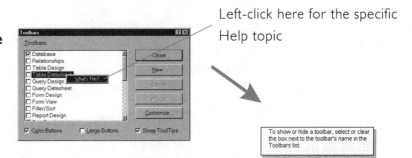

Other standard Windows 95 Help features are also present; see your Windows documentation for how to use these.

Access also has one additional Help feature: the Answer Wizard. Answer Wizard is more or less unique to Microsoft Office applications.

The Answer Wizard (1)

Access' Help armoury has an additional weapon you can use: the Answer Wizard.

Often, when you invoke Help within Access, you know more or less the question you want to ask, or the topic on which you need information. But what happens if neither of these is true?

Use the Answer Wizard to get round this difficulty. Its purpose is to allow you to enter questions *in your own terminology*. If you don't know the correct term for what you want to ask, you can put the question in your own words. The Answer Wizard then provides a list of available topics from which you can choose.

You can also launch the Answer Wizard by clicking the Answer Wizard button in the Contents and Index windows.

There are various methods you can use to launch the Answer Wizard.

Launching Answer Wizard with the Help menu
Pull down the Help menu and do the following:

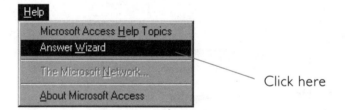

Launching Answer Wizard from within toolbars
(If an appropriate toolbar isn't currently visible on your screen, follow the procedures listed in the Toolbars (1) topic earlier.)

Do the following:

The ⓚ? button is found in nearly all Access toolbars.

The Answer Wizard (2)

Launching Answer Wizard with the Shortcut bar

If you have other components of Microsoft Office installed on your system (including the Shortcut bar), activate the Office section of the bar and do the following:

Click here

Using the Answer Wizard

Carry out the following procedures:

Type in your question or topic, then click Search

Double-click the appropriate Help entry

Access now launches the relevant Help window. When you've finished using this, press Esc or Alt+F4 to close it.

Closing down Access

It's easy to shut down Access when you've finished using it in a particular editing session.

To exit Access when you're through using it, pull down the File menu and do the following:

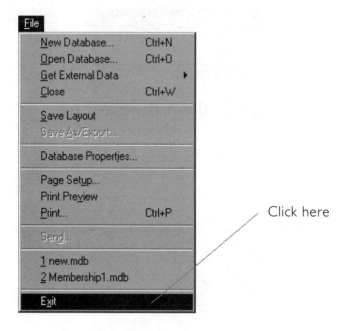

Click here

Alternatively, press Alt+F4, or click the Close button ☒ on the far right of the Access Title bar.

When you close down Access, you're warned if you've made changes to open databases without saving them. Do one of the following:

2 Click here to close Access *without* saving your data

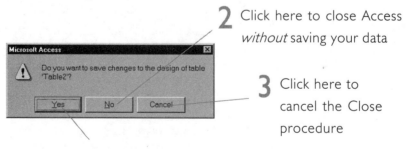

3 Click here to cancel the Close procedure

Click here to save your data *and* close Access

CHAPTER TWO

Your first database

This chapter shows you how to create new databases. First, we'll discuss elements you need to sort out *before* you start. Then you'll learn how to create a simple database manually, and also how to create more complex examples by automating the process with Database Wizards. Finally, you'll discover how to open databases you've already created, and how to save your work.

Covers

Database terminology

Before you can learn to use Access to create databases, you need to be familiar with and understand the following terms:

Database	Information grouped together (and organised for ease of reference) into an Access file
Tables	Used to store data in rows and columns, like a spreadsheet
Records	(Horizontal) rows of data in tables. Each record is a complete set of related data items (for instance, in a magazine's subscription database each record is the information associated with each subscriber)
Fields	(Vertical) columns of data in tables. Fields are spaces reserved for specified data (for instance, subscription payment details for all records in a magazine database might be kept in a field called 'Renewals')

REMEMBER

This is an extract from a table associated with the MEMBERSHIP Wizard. It's filled with sample data, for illustration purposes.

Fields

First Name	Last Name	Home Address	City
Karl	Jablonski	722 DaVinci Bl	Kirkland
Elizabeth	Lincoln	1900 Oak St.	Vancouver
Nancy	Davolio	507 - 20th Ave.	Seattle
Janet	Leverling	4110 Old Redm	Redmond
Laura	Callahan	4726 - 11th Ave	Seattle
Steven	Buchanan	Coventry House	London
Hari	Kumar	90 Wadhurst R	London
Patricio	Simpson	Cerrito 333	Buenos Aires
Yoshi	Latimer	2732 Baker Blv	Eugene
Lino	Rodriguez	Estrada da saú	Lisboa
Art	Braunschweiger		
Robert	King	7 Houndstooth F	London

Records

... contd

Query   The process by which data can be extracted from tables in accordance with criteria you specify. Queries represent ways of viewing fields from more than one table or query in the same record

This is an extract from a form associated with the MEMBERSHIP Wizard. It's filled with sample data, for illustration purposes.

Forms   You use forms to display table or query data in a customised format. As with queries, forms can host information from one or more tables or queries

Fields

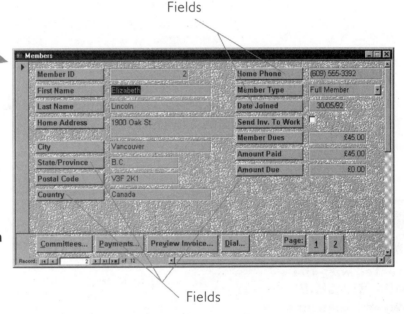

Fields

Forms display one record at a time, and are often the most convenient way to interact with your data.

Tables, queries, forms and reports are all 'objects'. In Access, objects are items which can be selected and manipulated.

Reports   Use reports to display table or query data in a customised format (with page numbers and headings). Reports can't be edited, but they can contain data from one or more tables or queries

The pre-planning stage

Before you start to create a database, it's a good idea to plan it out first. This can save you a lot of time and effort. Consider implementing the following suggestions:

- If you'll be basing your new database on an existing one (manual or computerised), study the ways in which your data is currently organised. This will help when it comes to creating Access tables and queries.

- Make sure you're clear in your own mind about the categories into which data can be split logically. For example, a magazine would clearly wish to have a section where subscription details were maintained, and arguably a separate section for payment details.

- Plan out which fields you want your new database to have. For example, a magazine (and most other database types) would need fields relating to:

  - Client names

  - Addresses

  - Phone numbers

A table excerpt from a database created with the MEMBERSHIP Wizard; logically, this field could be the primary key:

- Determine which fields within specific tables can serve as 'primary keys'. The primary key is the field which is common to each record, and which identifies it as being unique. In our magazine example, this could well be the Member ID field. Primary keys are also used by Access to determine the order in which records are sorted, and to speed up the processing of queries.

Member ID	First Name	Last Name	Home Address
1	Kiri	Jablonski	722 DaVinci Blv
2	Elizabeth	Lincoln	1900 Oak St.
3	Nancy	Davolio	507 - 20th Ave.
4	Janet	Leverling	4110 Old Redm
5	Laura	Callahan	4726 - 11th Ave
6	Steven	Buchanan	Coventry House
7	Hari	Kumar	90 Wadhurst R
8	Patricio	Simpson	Cerrito 333
9	Yoshi	Latimer	2732 Baker Blv
10	Lino	Rodriguez	Estrada da saú
11	Art	Braunschweiger	
12	Robert	King	7 Houndstooth
(AutoNumber)			

Creating databases - an overview

There are two ways to create new databases in Access:

- using an appropriate wizard

- manually

Both approaches have their merits. The manual method provides more precision: you create a blank database and then include the necessary components over a period of time. This method gives you complete control over the make-up of your database, but the process can easily become long-winded. The various 'Starting Access' topics in Chapter 1 show you how to use this technique to create a very simple database *at the same time as you start Access*. (Or see the 'Creating databases manually' topics later for how to do this when Access is already running.)

 See the techniques discussed in later chapters for how to customise and supplement manually created databases.

The wizard method, on the other hand, is much easier to use, far more convenient and just as effective. You can select and apply the Database Wizard you need (there are 22 to choose from). When you do so, the wizard automatically inserts the necessary objects in accordance with your specifications.

Database Wizards let you specify:

- the overall form background (you can choose from 10 preset colours and patterns)

- report styles

- which tables and fields should be included

- an overall database title

Although they don't permit the same complexity as the manual method, wizards do have the advantage of creating databases which are tailor-made for the purpose for which they were designed. They represent a fast, convenient and detailed method for the creation of databases.

Whichever method you use to create a database, you can easily amend it later.

Creating databases manually (1)

For how to create a database manually *just after you've launched Access, see the 'Starting Access' topics in Chapter 1.*

To create a database manually from within Access, pull down the File menu and click New Database. Now do the following:

1 Make sure the General tab is active

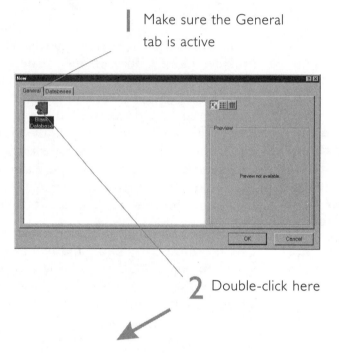

2 Double-click here

3 Click here; select the drive/folder you want to host the new database

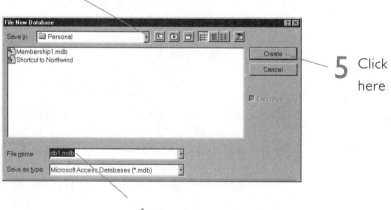

5 Click here

4 Type in a name

Creating databases manually (2)

There are two further dialogs which have to be negotiated. After step 3 below, Access creates a database table. (But see the tip below for help with automating the entire process of table creation.)

Click here

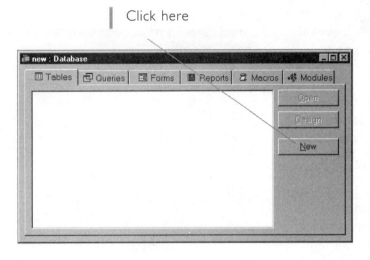

HANDY TIP **Re step 2 - at this point you can, if you want to, automate the creation of a table with the use of a wizard. See the 'Automating table creation' topics in Chapter 3 for how to do this.**

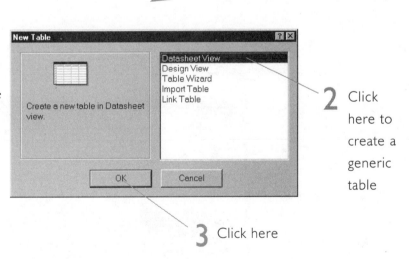

2 Click here to create a generic table

3 Click here

Automating database creation (1)

To create a database with the help of the Database Wizard, pull down the File menu and click New Database. Now do the following:

REMEMBER

Database Wizards consist of several stages, each represented by a specific dialog. The precise content varies somewhat from wizard to wizard. The ADDRESS BOOK Wizard produces a less complex database than others.

1 Ensure the Databases tab is active

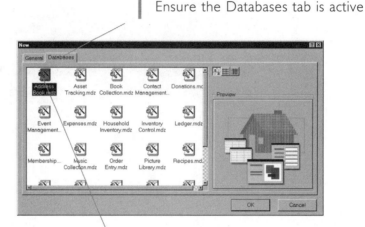

2 Double-click the appropriate database type

3 Click here; select the drive/folder you want to host the new database

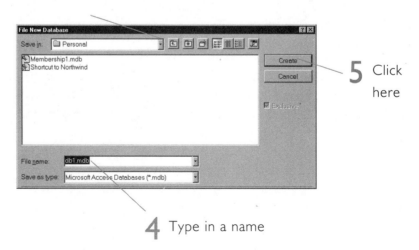

5 Click here

4 Type in a name

Automating database creation (2)

Access launches additional dialogs. Complete them as follows:

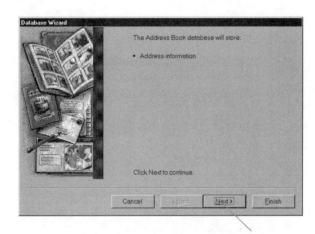

Some wizards provide more than one table here: If this is the case, click the table which hosts fields you want to include in your database, *then* **carry out steps 2 & 3.**

Click here

2 Click the fields you want to include

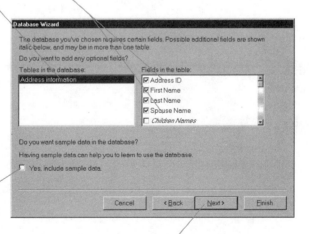

Click here to include sample data in the database (this can help you familiarise yourself with how to use it).

3 Click here

Automating database creation (3)

The following additional dialogs launch. Complete them as follows:

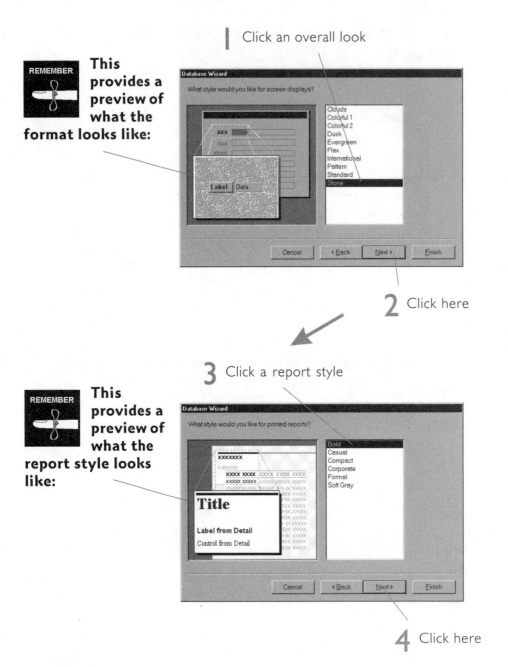

Click an overall look

This provides a preview of what the format looks like:

2 Click here

3 Click a report style

This provides a preview of what the report style looks like:

4 Click here

Automating database creation (4)

These are the final dialogs in the Database Wizard. Carry out the following steps:

| Type in a database title

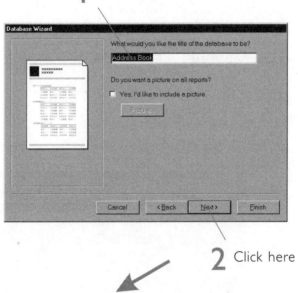

2 Click here

3 Ensure this is selected to have Access open the new database automatically

After step 4, Access creates the new database. The process can sometimes take a little while...

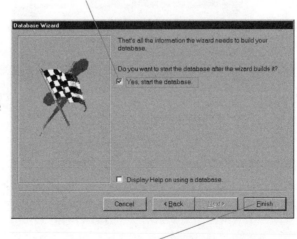

4 Click here

Opening existing databases (1)

We've just seen how Access lets you create new databases in various ways. Once you've done this, you'll need to open them for editing. You can open existing databases:

HANDY TIP

You can also use the Documents section of the Windows 95 Startup menu to open recently used Access files - see your Windows 95 documentation for how to do this.

- in the process of starting Access

- from within Access

Opening a database at startup
Immediately after you've started Access, carry out steps 1 and 2, or 1 and 3, as appropriate:

Click here

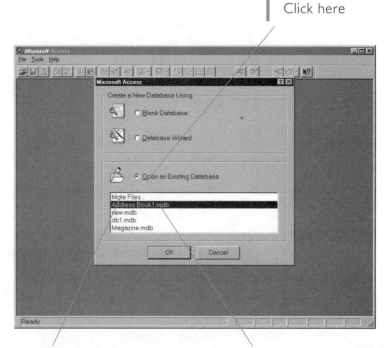

3 Double-click here if the existing file you need isn't shown in step 2

2 Double-click a recently used file to open it

If you follow steps 1 and 3, the Open dialog appears. See page 33 for how to complete this.

Opening existing databases (2)

Opening a database from within Access

Pull down the File menu and click Open. Now carry out the following steps, as appropriate:

You can use a keyboard shortcut to launch the Open dialog: simply press Ctrl+O.

2 Click here. In the drop-down list, click the drive/folder which hosts the file

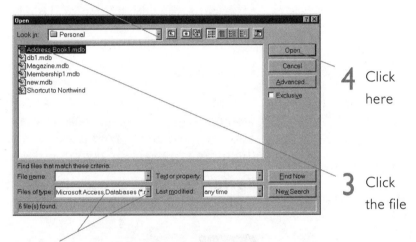

4 Click here

3 Click the file

Make sure Microsoft Access Databases is shown. If it isn't, click the arrow and select it from the drop-down list

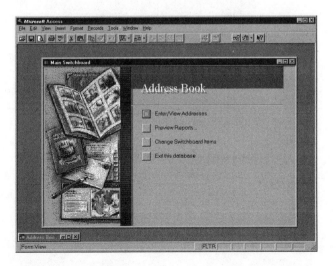

The opened database

Saving operations

Most programs require you to save your work at frequent intervals, in order to avoid data loss in the event of a hardware fault or power interruption. However, Access does this for you. Access automatically saves the record you're working on whenever you:

- move the insertion point to a different record

- close the active form or datasheet

- close the relevant database

- close down Access itself

You can also save your work manually, if you want (for instance, if you suspect that Windows 95 is about to crash). You can save the active record, or the complete database (including the various layout and design components).

Saving the active record
Pull down the Records menu and do the following:

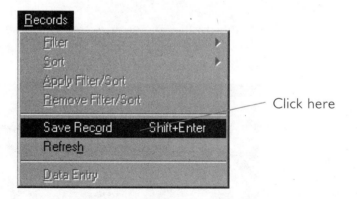

Click here

Saving databases
To save the whole database, pull down the File menu and click Save.

Creating tables

This chapter shows you how to create new tables. First, you'll learn how to automate the process with a wizard. Then you'll discover how to create a simple table manually. You'll create your own fields, allocate data types to them and customise field properties. Finally, you'll save your work to disk.

Covers

Tables - an overview

After you've created an Access database, the next step is to create the tables which store your data. This is essential if you created the database manually (if you used a Database Wizard to create your database, you'll already have one or more tailor-made tables ready to use – even then, however, you'll probably want to create your own at some time). The procedures outlined in this chapter apply to both scenarios.

All other objects in Access databases (e.g. forms, queries and reports) are predicated on the data contained in tables.

There are two basic ways to create a table:

- manually

- with the help of the Table Wizard

Both approaches certainly have their merits. On the one hand, the manual method provides more precision: you create a blank table and then (in a separate operation) include whatever fields you wish. You can also customise the field formats. This method gives you complete control over the make-up of your table, but the overall process is relatively time-consuming.

The wizard method, on the other hand, is much easier to use, and far more convenient. You can:

- choose from a selection of table types

- choose from a selection of table designs

- enter data into the table

- enter data into a form created by the Wizard

Although using the Table Wizard doesn't permit the same complexity as the manual method, it does represent a fast, convenient, detailed and effective method for the creation of tables.

Whichever method you use to create a table, you can easily amend it later.

The Database window

When you create a new database in Access (or open an existing one), the Database window displays. Since this is the basis for table creation, we need to discuss this before we move on.

The illustration below shows a small, manually created database:

Magnified view of Close button

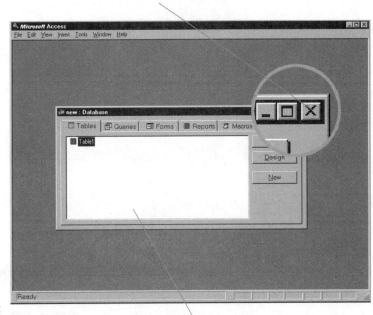

Database window

The Database window may appear as a minimised bar in the bottom left-hand corner of the screen:

Click here to restore (expand) it.

The Database window can be thought of as a command centre for the active database. For example, clicking on the Close button closes the database. It's also the basis from which much of the work you carry out with tables, queries, forms and reports is undertaken.

Automating table creation (1)

To create a table with the help of the Table Wizard, first make sure that the Database window is visible (see the 'Database window' topic earlier for how to do this). Then do the following:

Activate the Tables tab

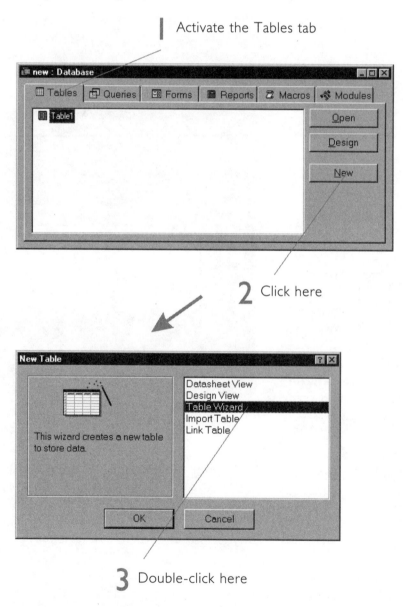

2 Click here

3 Double-click here

Automating table creation (2)

Access now launches the Table Wizard. Do the following:

2 Click a sample table

3 Double-click the fields you want to include

If you want to rename fields, click the Rename Field button just after you've carried out step 3.

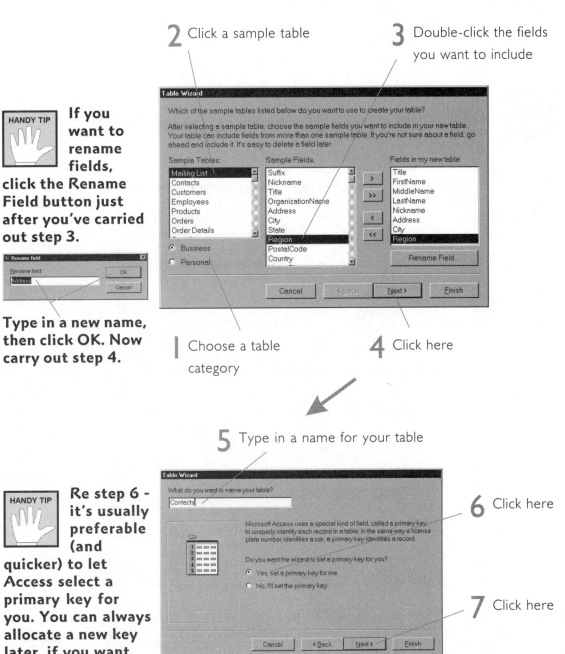

Type in a new name, then click OK. Now carry out step 4.

| Choose a table category

4 Click here

5 Type in a name for your table

Re step 6 - it's usually preferable (and quicker) to let Access select a primary key for you. You can always allocate a new key later, if you want.

6 Click here

7 Click here

Automating table creation (3)

The next stage in the process of table creation has to do with relationships. Often, when you build a new table one or more of the records will be held in common with other tables. When this is so, you need to tell Access what the precise relationship is.

If your new table has no common records, simply omit steps 1-3 inclusive. Instead, merely follow step 4.

Do the following:

1 Click here if your new table is related to another

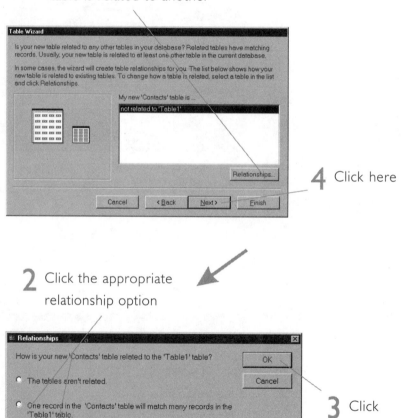

4 Click here

2 Click the appropriate relationship option

3 Click here

Automating table creation (4)

The Table Wizard is now almost ready to create your table. When it's done so, you'll probably want to begin entering data more or less immediately. Access lets you do this in two ways:

- directly into the table

- into a form built by the wizard

You can also opt to have Access let you customise the design of your table when the wizard has completed it. See the 'Amending table design' topics (et al) later for how to do this.

Each of these techniques has its own particular merits; you can specify which you prefer now.

The table method is more suitable for the rapid entering of information in bulk, while the form method is more visually appealing and – arguably – makes your data easier to work with.

Carry out the following steps:

Click a data entry option

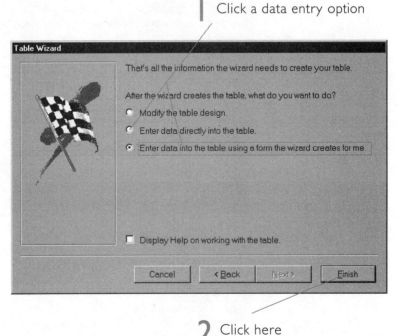

2 Click here

Automating table creation (5)

The Table Wizard now launches one of the following (according to the option you chose in step 1 in the 'Automating table creation (4)' topic earlier):

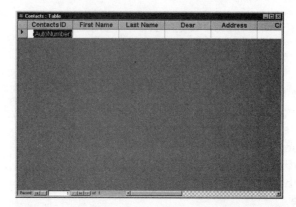

A table containing a single blank record

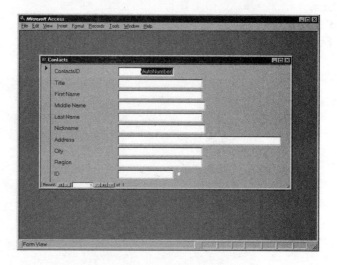

A form showing the first (blank) record in the new table

You can now begin entering data into your new table. (For how to do this, see Chapter 5).

Creating tables manually

To create a table from scratch, first make sure that the Database window is visible (see the 'Database window' topic earlier for how to do this). Then carry out the following steps:

1 Activate the Tables tab

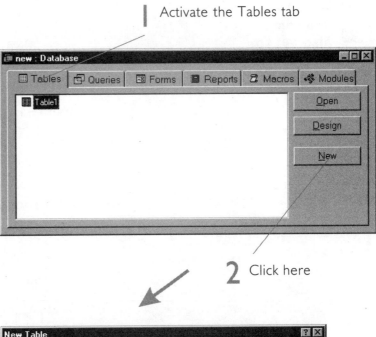

2 Click here

After step 3, Access creates the new table:

See the 'Amending table design' topics later (et al) for how to customise it.

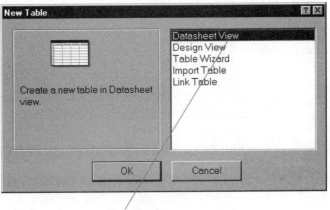

3 Double-click here

Table design - an overview

Now that you've created a table manually, you need to customise the field conformation. This involves specifying the following information:

If you want to, you can also opt to redesign tables created with the Table Wizard.

- names

- data types

- format/field size

- additional field properties

You can choose from several data types. The main ones are:

Text	Use for text and numbers which don't require calculations performed on them (e.g. phone numbers)
Memo	Use for annotations (text and numbers)
Number	Use for calculable numbers
Date/Time	Use for dates (within the year range 100 to 9,999) and times
Currency	Self-explanatory
AutoNumber	Access uses this to identify records automatically and sequentially

The field properties you can set depend on the data type allocated. For example, in fields which have had Text allocated as a data type you can specify (among other features) the maximum number of characters data entries can have. On the other hand, if Date/Time is the data type, you can choose from a variety of date and time formats (e.g. '12 May 1996' or '12/05/96').

Another example: if you allocate Number as the data type, you can set the number of decimal places Access uses to display numbers in the relevant field, and you can determine whether scientific notation is used (e.g. 2.16E +03).

Amending table design (1)

There are two ways to begin customising a table's design.

If the table is already open
Pull down the View menu and do the following:

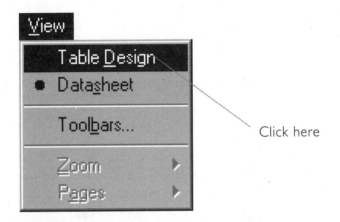

Click here

If the table isn't already open
Go to the Database window (see the 'The Database window' topic earlier for how to do this) and do the following:

Activate the Tables tab

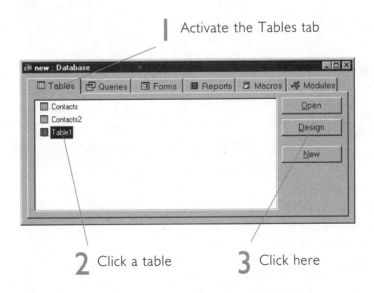

2 Click a table   3 Click here

Amending table design (2)

The Table Design window now launches. This is the basis for adding and customising fields. There are two sections:

- the Field Format pane

- the Field Properties pane

Field Format pane

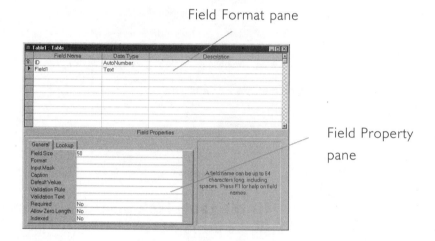

Field Property pane

Applying a name and data type

Before you can specify field characteristics, you need to name the new field and apply a data type.

In this instance, the first field in the Table Design table (it enters a unique ID reference automatically) was inserted by Access and needs no reformatting.

Do the following:

Type in a name

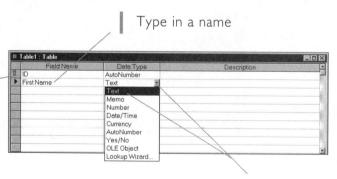

2 Click here; select a data type in the list

Setting Text properties (1)

When a field has the Text data type associated with it, you may need to specify:

The character limit

The character maximum for Text fields is 255; often, fields will benefit from having far fewer (one benefit is that Access processes them more quickly).

 The next few topics explore the main customisation options which result from specific data types.

A caption

'Captions' in Access are special titles which only display in forms.

A default value

Default values are text and/or numerals which you want to appear in every instance of the field (e.g. you might wish the Country field in a Contacts database to show 'U.K.' permanently).

Indexing

Implementing indexing in a database often (but not always) enables Access to find and sort records faster (if it knows where information is, it can usually reach it more rapidly). Indexing only applies to the Text, Number, Currency and Date/Time data types. Fields which have had a primary key allocated are automatically indexed. When you index a field, you can specify whether duplicated values are allowed; for instance, you may want to allow duplicate names in a 'Surname' field.

 You should index fields you use frequently, and which contain a wide variety of data. An obvious choice for most databases would be the field which contains surname details.

Setting Text properties (2)

Launch the Table Design window (see the 'Amending Table design (1) topic for how to do this). Then carry out any of steps 1-4 below. If you carry out step 4, also follow step 5 OR 6:

1 Type in a character limit

2 Type in a caption

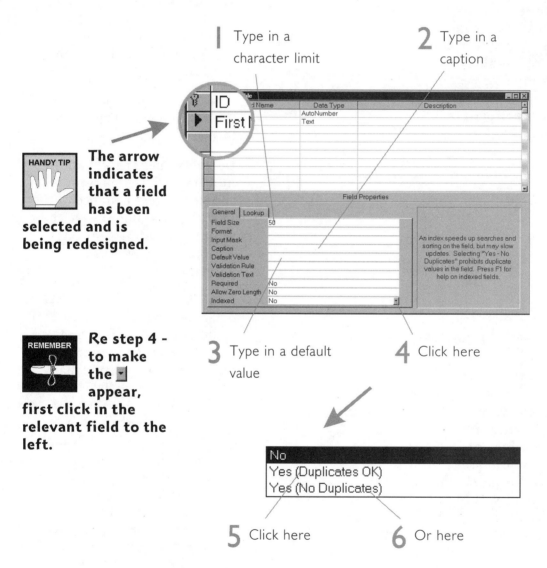

HANDY TIP **The arrow indicates that a field has been selected and is being redesigned.**

REMEMBER **Re step 4 – to make the ▾ appear, first click in the relevant field to the left.**

3 Type in a default value

4 Click here

| No |
| Yes (Duplicates OK) |
| Yes (No Duplicates) |

5 Click here

6 Or here

Setting Number properties (1)

If you set a field's data type to Number, features you can specify include:

Field Size

You can choose from a variety of settings. The main ones are:

Integer – stores *whole* numbers in the range -32,768 to 32,768

Long Integer – stores *whole* numbers in the range -2,147,483,648 to +2,147,483,647

Single – stores numbers in the range -3.402823E38 to +3.402823E38

 REMEMBER

You can also set properties that have already been discussed. For example, you can index fields which have had the Number data type applied.

Format

You can specify the number format for a field's contents. The main choices are:

General Number – numbers display as entered

Fixed – numbers display with two decimal places

Standard – as Fixed, but Access denotes thousands with a comma (e.g. 3,267.12)

Percent – Access multiplies inserted values by 100 and adds '%'

Decimal Places

You can specify how many places numerical values should be expressed to.

The acceptable range is 0 to 15.

Setting Number properties (2)

Launch the Table Design window (see the 'Amending table design (1) topic for how to do this). Then carry out any of steps 1-3 below. If you carry out step 1, also follow step 4. Steps 2 and 3 should be followed by 5 and 6 respectively:

Re steps 1, 2 and 3 - to make the ⬛ appear, first click in the relevant field to the left.

Click here

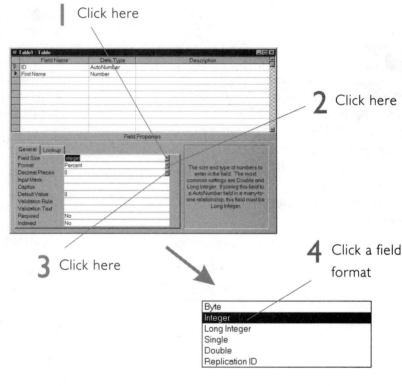

2 Click here

3 Click here

4 Click a field format

Steps 4, 5 and 6 show subsidiary windows which launch according to whether you follow steps 1, 2 or 3.

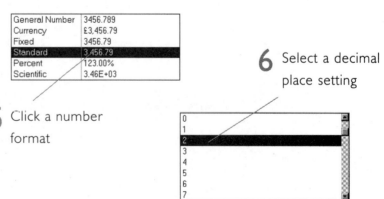

| Byte |
| Integer |
| Long Integer |
| Single |
| Double |
| Replication ID |

General Number	3456.789
Currency	£3,456.79
Fixed	3456.79
Standard	3,456.79
Percent	123.00%
Scientific	3.46E+03

6 Select a decimal place setting

5 Click a number format

| 0 |
| 1 |
| 2 |
| 3 |
| 4 |
| 5 |
| 6 |
| 7 |

Setting Date/Time properties (1)

If you set a field's data type to Date/Time, there are fewer available features (and many of them have already been discussed in earlier topics). However, you do need to be familiar with the following:

Format

You can specify the date and/or time formats for a field's contents. The choices are:

General Date – displays dates and/or times as Windows 95 itself does (e.g. 05/06/96 09:00:12)

Short Date – same as the date component of the General Date option

Medium Date – a halfway house (e.g. 01-Apr-1996)

Long Date – shows dates in full (e.g. Sunday, May 19, 1996)

Short Time – shows times as an irreducible minimum (e.g. 13.45)

Medium Time – displays slightly more information than the Short Time option, and doesn't use the 24-hour clock (e.g. 08:32 PM)

Long Time – same as the time component of the General Date option

Setting Date/Time properties (2)

Launch the Table Design window (see the 'Amending table design (1) topic for how to do this). Then carry out steps 1 and 2 below:

Click here

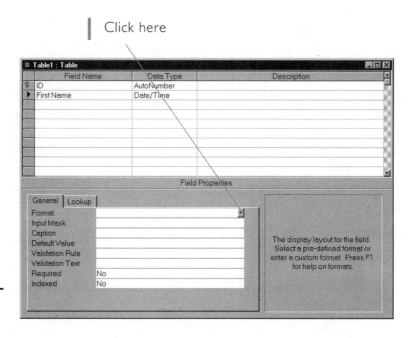

**Re step 1 -
to make
the**
**appear,
first click in the
relevant field to the
left.**

General Date	19/06/94 17:34:23
Long Date	19 June 1994
Medium Date	19-Jun-94
Short Date	19/06/94
Long Time	17:34:23
Medium Time	05:34 PM
Short Time	17:34

2 Click a
Date/Time
format

Setting Currency properties

When you allocate Currency as a field's data type, many of the options are more or less identical with those associated with Number. For instance, you can allocate the same Format and Decimal Place options.

Launch the Table Design window (see the 'Amending table design (1) topic for how to do this). Then carry out steps 1 and 2 below, followed by steps 3 OR 4 respectively:

Re steps 1 and 2 - to make the ⬛ appear, first click in the relevant field to the left.

Click here

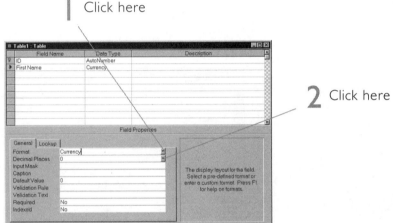

2 Click here

Steps 3 and 4 show subsidiary windows which launch according to whether you follow step 1 or 2.

3 Click a number format

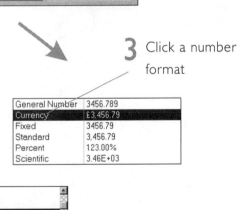

4 Select a decimal place setting

Saving your design work

When you've finished designing table fields, it's necessary to save your work to disk. This is a two-stage process and involves:

- closing the Table Design window

- responding appropriately to a warning message

Do the following:

Click here

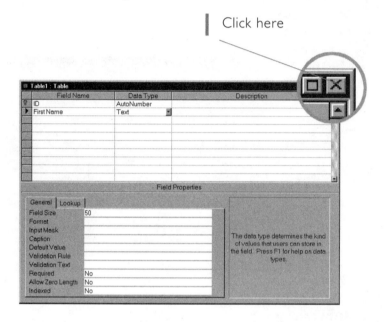

 Click here

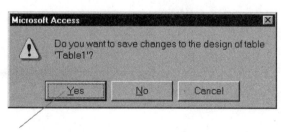

CHAPTER FOUR

Creating forms

This chapter shows you how to create new forms. First, you'll learn how to automate the process with AutoForm and a wizard. Then you'll discover how to create a simple form manually. You'll apply preset format schemes to it, add fields and labels, and customise field and label formats individually. Finally, you'll save your work to disk.

Covers

Forms - an overview

Once you've created an Access database and (possibly one or more tables to go with it), you may well wish to create forms to view your data in a more 'user-friendly' way. If you used a Database Wizard to create your database, you'll already have one or more tailor-made forms ready to use (even then, however, you may well want to create your own at some time). If, on the other hand, you created the database manually, you'll have to create any forms you need. The procedures outlined in this chapter apply to both scenarios.

There are three ways to create a form:

AutoForm is a kind of 'mini-wizard'; it produces simplified forms automatically, based on existing database tables.

- using AutoForm

- with the help of a Form Wizard

- manually

All three approaches have their merits. On the one hand, the manual method provides more precision: you create a blank form and then (in a separate operation) include whatever fields you wish. You can also customise the field formats. This method gives you complete control over the make-up of your form, but the overall process is relatively time-consuming.

The wizard/AutoForm methods, on the other hand, are far easier to use. For instance, the Form Wizard lets you:

- choose from three form layouts

- choose from a selection of form styles

- specify which tables/fields are included

Although using AutoForm or the Form Wizard doesn't permit the same complexity as the manual method, it does represent a fast, convenient, detailed and effective method for the creation of forms.

Whichever method you use to create a form, you can easily amend it later.

Using AutoForm

To create a form with Access' AutoForm feature, first make sure that the Database window is visible. (See 'The Database window' topic in Chapter 3 for how to do this.) Then do the following:

 In forms created with AutoForm, all fields and records in the selected table display. Each field appears on a separate line.

| Activate the Tables tab

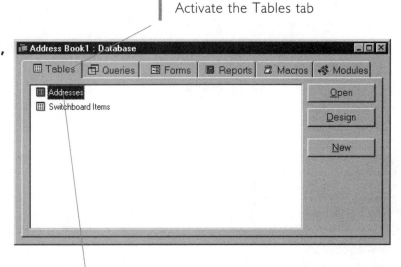

 This is the Database toolbar. Most toolbars contain the (New Object) button.

2 Double-click the table on which you want to base the form

3 Click here

4 Click here

Automating form creation (1)

To create a form with the help of the Form Wizard, first make sure that the Database window is visible (see 'The Database window' topic in Chapter 3 for how to do this). Then do the following:

Activate the Forms tab

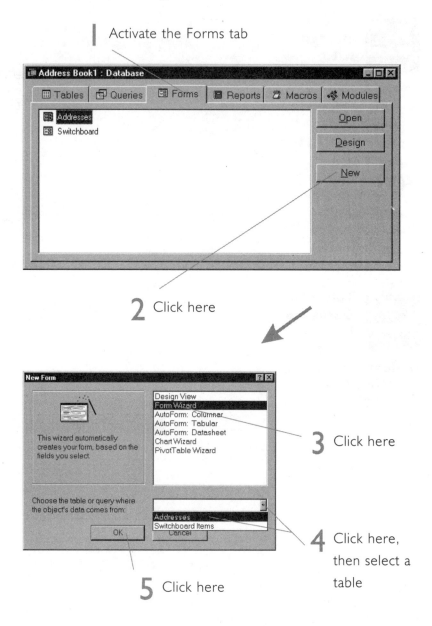

2 Click here

3 Click here

4 Click here, then select a table

5 Click here

Automating form creation (2)

Access now launches the Form Wizard. Carry out the following steps:

| Double-click the fields you want to include

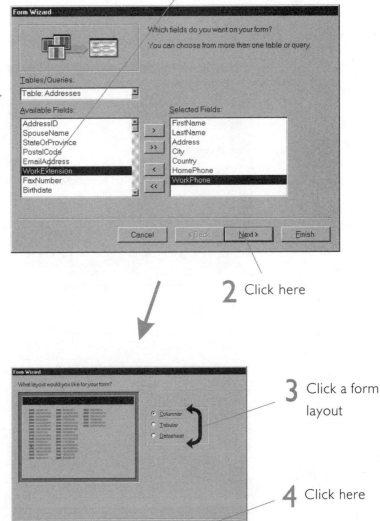

 HANDY TIP

Re step 1 - when you carried out step 4 in the 'Automating form creation (1)' topic, you selected a table on which to base the new form. If you want to use fields from *additional* tables, click here:

Tables/Queries:

Then select a new table from the list. Finally, carry out steps 2-4.

2 Click here

3 Click a form layout

4 Click here

Automating form creation (3)

In the final stage of the process of form creation, you select the overall style you want your new form to have. This is especially important in the case of forms because they're highly visual.

Do the following:

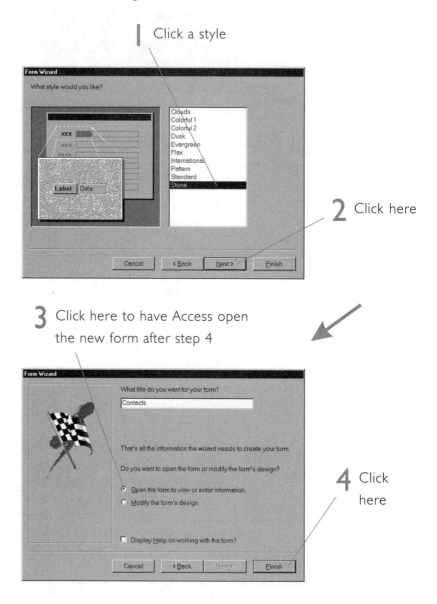

Click a style

2 Click here

3 Click here to have Access open the new form after step 4

4 Click here

Automating form creation (4)

The Form Wizard now creates your new form. It then opens it for editing.

The illustrations below show two varieties of form (according to whether you selected AutoForm: Columnar or AutoForm: Tabular as the basic layout in step 3 in the 'Automating form creation (1)' topic earlier):

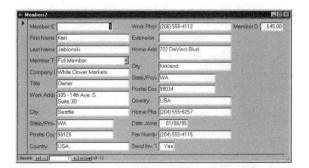

The Columnar form

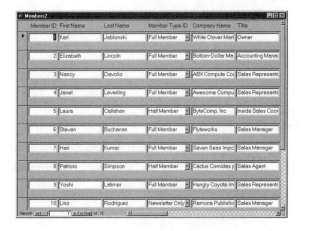

The Tabular form

Whichever form layout you selected, you can now begin entering data into your new form. (For how to do this, see Chapter 5.)

Creating forms manually

To create a form from scratch, first make sure that the Database window is visible. (See 'The Database window' topic in Chapter 3 for how to do this.) Then carry out the following steps:

1 | Activate the Forms tab

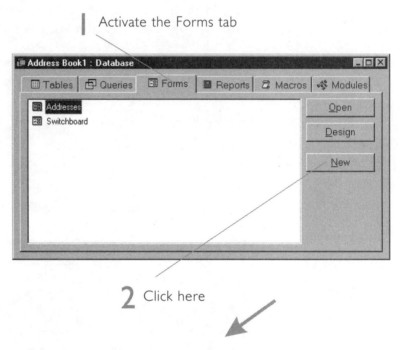

2 Click here

After step 4, Access creates the new form. See the 'Amending form design' topics later (et al) for how to customise it.

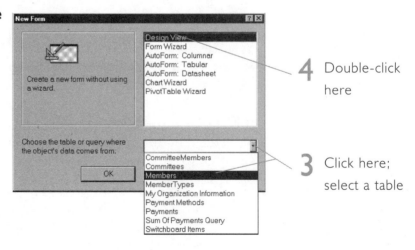

4 Double-click here

3 Click here; select a table

Form design - an overview

Now that you've created a form manually, you must add the various fields and labels (explanatory classifications) you need. Access calls everything you add to a form a 'control'. There are two main types:

- bound

- unbound

Bound controls pull in data from fields in an underlying database table. For instance, if a field in a table contains post code information, the relevant control will return post code data for the currently active record.

Unbound controls, on the other hand, contain supplementary text (e.g. instructions to the database user) or graphics components (e.g. lines); they aren't connected to table fields.

The distinction is made clear in the following:

HANDY TIP If you want to, you can also opt to redesign forms created with the Form Wizard.

HANDY TIP To see what your work looks like, now or at any stage in the form design process, pull down the View menu and click Form. To continue your design work, pull down the same menu and click Form Design.

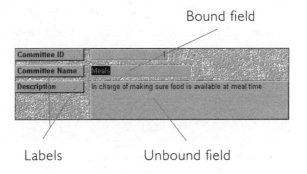

Bound field

Labels

Unbound field

Bound & unbound fields in a form extract

Bound field

The bound field in the original table

Customising form design is much more visual than customising tables.

Amending form design (1)

There are two ways to begin customising a form's design.

If the form is already open
Pull down the View menu and do the following:

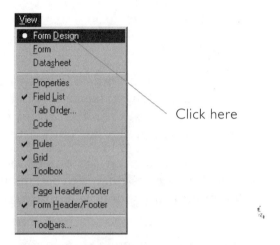

Click here

If the form isn't already open
Go to the Database window (see 'The Database window' topic in Chapter 3 for how to do this) and do the following:

Activate the Forms tab

2 Click a form   3 Click here

Amending form design (2)

Access now launches the form in Form Design view. This is the basis for adding and customising fields. The following components are especially important:

- the Detail pane
- the Toolbox
- the Field List

HANDY TIP

If the Field List isn't currently visible, pull down the View menu and click Field List.

Detail pane

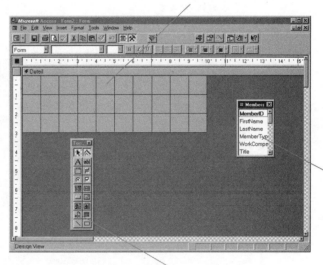

Field List

Toolbox

HANDY TIP

You can resize the Detail pane. Move the mouse pointer over a side or corner (the pointer changes to a 4-pronged arrow). Click and drag appropriately. Release the button to confirm the operation.

The Detail pane represents the current body of your form. Here, you create and design the necessary fields.

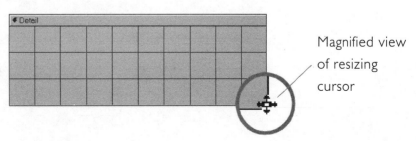

Magnified view of resizing cursor

AutoFormat

Access provides a way to apply a series of pre-defined formats to overall form design. Use AutoFormat to impose:

- a background

- a preset control font

- a preset control border

Using AutoFormat

Do the following to select the entire form:

Click here

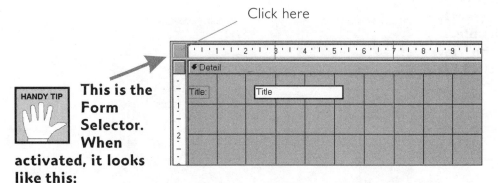

HANDY TIP

This is the Form Selector. When activated, it looks like this:

Now pull down the Format menu and click AutoFormat. Carry out the following steps:

Double-click a style

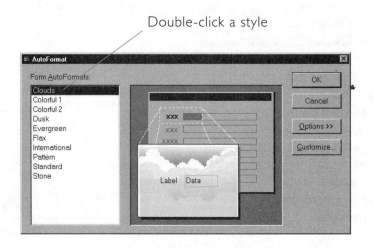

Adding labels (1)

It's useful to add descriptive labels to forms. You can add labels to:

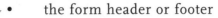

- the form header or footer

- the Detail pane

First, refer to the Form toolbox and do the following:

HANDY TIP **If you want to add a label to a header or footer and the form header/footer area isn't currently visible, do the following. In Form Design view, pull down the View menu and click Form Header/ Footer.**

Click here

Move the pointer to the appropriate location in the header/ footer or Detail pane. Hold down the left mouse button and drag to define the label area:

Label area

REMEMBER **This magnified view shows how the cursor changes when you're defining a label:**

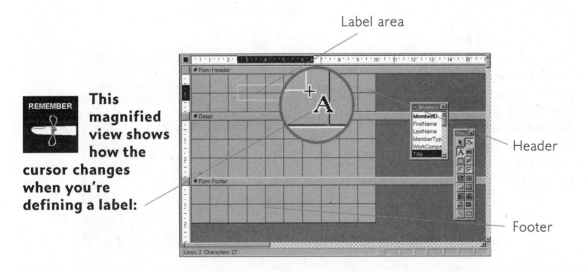

Header

Footer

Release the mouse button to complete the label.

Adding labels (2)

So far, your label looks something like this:

Label

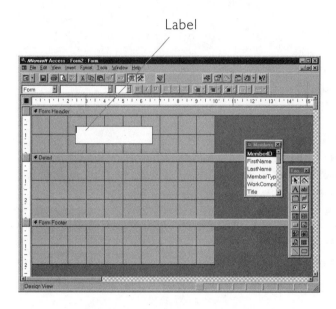

The next stage is to type in the label text. When you've finished, press Enter.

HANDY TIP

You'll probably need to reformat most labels after you've created them. See the 'Reformatting labels and fields' topic later for how to do this.

The inserted label

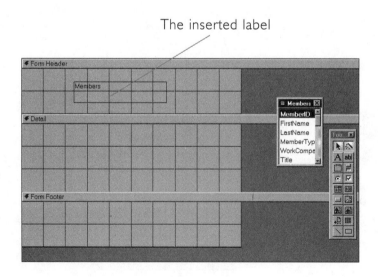

Adding fields

Once you've inserted the necessary labels, the next stage is to insert the required fields. This is a simple process involving a drag-and-drop technique.

In Form Design view, make sure the Field List is visible. (If it isn't, pull down the View menu and click Field List.) Then do the following:

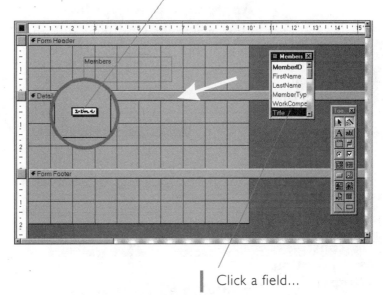

2 Drag it to the appropriate location in the form

Click a field...

Fields in forms consist of two parts:

• **the field name:**

• **the field detail:**

Title

Release the mouse button to insert the new field.

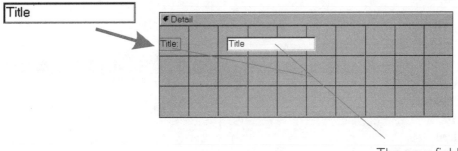

The new field

Reformatting labels and fields (1)

Once you've inserted a new label or field, you can:

- apply a new typeface and/or type size

- align the contents

- apply foreground and/or background colours

- specify a border width and/or colour

- apply special effects

You can select multiple controls by holding down Shift as you click them.

Applying a new typeface

First, select the control(s) you want to amend. Then do the following:

If you want to reformat the field name _as well as_ the field detail, don't forget to select it as well.

Formatting operations on controls use the Formatting (Form/Report Design) toolbar; it's automatically present in Form Design view.

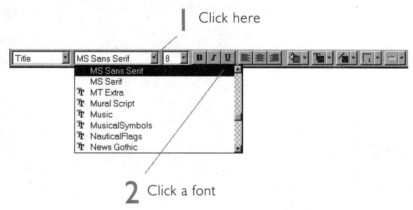

Click here

2 Click a font

Applying a new type size

First, select the control(s) you want to amend. Then do the following:

Click here

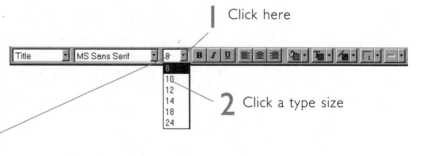

2 Click a type size

For greater precision, simply type in a new type size here: Then press Return.

Reformatting labels and fields (2)

Aligning label and field contents

First, select the control you want to amend by clicking it. (If you want to select more than one, hold down Shift at the same time.) Then carry out any of the following:

The figures below show alignment in action:

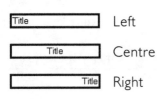

Left

Centre

Right

2 Click here to centre control contents

1 Click here to align contents to the left

3 Click here to align contents to the right

Colouring foregrounds and backgrounds

First, select the control you want to amend by clicking it. (If you want to select more than one, hold down Shift at the same time.) Then follow steps 1 AND 2 to apply a background colour, or 3 AND 4 to apply a foreground colour:

1 Click here

3 Click here

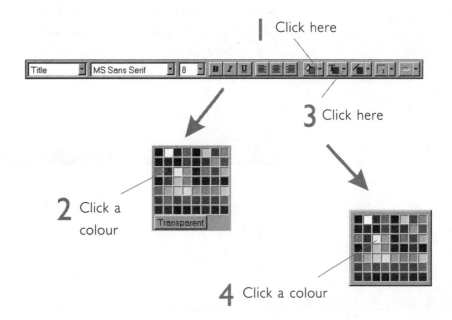

2 Click a colour

4 Click a colour

Reformatting labels and fields (3)

Specifying a border width

Access is supplied with a small number of pre-defined line widths which can be applied to controls. Note, however, that you can only apply the appropriate border to all four sides of a control: you can't specify which edges you border.

First, select the control you want to amend by clicking it. (If you want to select more than one, hold down Shift at the same time.) Then do the following:

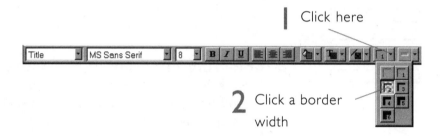

Click here

2 Click a border width

Specifying a border colour

First, select the control you want to amend by clicking it. (If you want to select more than one, hold down Shift at the same time.)

Then do the following:

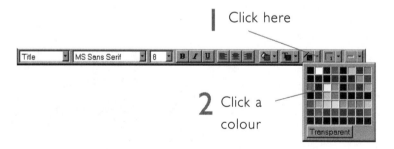

Click here

2 Click a colour

Reformatting labels and fields (4)

Applying special effects

Access lets you apply several special effects to controls. For instance, you can choose from:

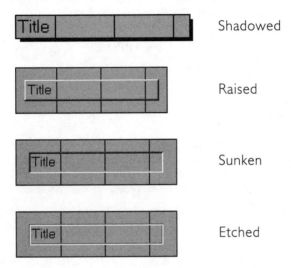

Shadowed

Raised

Sunken

Etched

First, select the control you want to amend by clicking it. (If you want to select more than one, hold down Shift at the same time.) Then do the following:

Click here

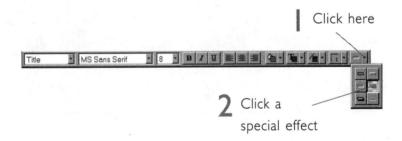

2 Click a special effect

Saving your form design

When you've finished designing your form, it's necessary to save your work to disk. This is a two-stage process and involves:

- closing down your form

- responding appropriately to a warning message

Do the following:

To avoid data loss, you should also save your work *on-the-fly*. To do this, simply press Ctrl+S at frequent intervals.

Click here

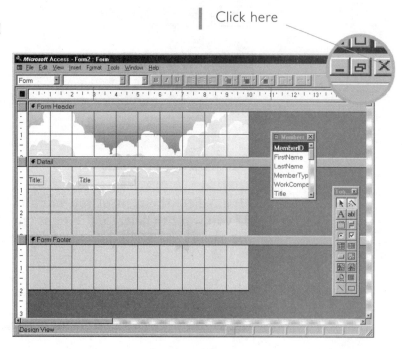

2 Click here

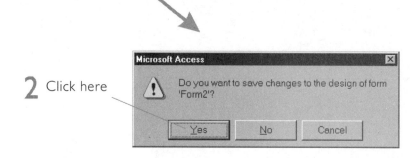

CHAPTER FIVE

Viewing and editing data

This chapter shows you how to interact with your data in Access views. Then you'll learn how to insert new records, as a prelude to entering data. You'll discover how to find your way around in databases, and how to amend existing data (including record deletion). You'll search for specific data, and sort it alphanumerically for convenience. Finally, you'll learn how to filter databases, and save your filter to disk for future use.

Covers

Using views - an overview

In Chapters 3 and 4, we looked at how to create and customise tables and designs. These operations take place in special Views known as Table Design and Form Design. These can be thought of as subsets of the following:

Datasheet view

Datasheet view presents your data in a grid structure reminiscent of a typical spreadsheet, with the columns denoting fields and the rows individual records.

Use Datasheet view for bulk data entry or comparison.

Form

Form view limits the display to one record at a time, while presenting it in a way which is more visual and therefore easier on the eye. The basis of this view is the 'form', the underlying database layout which you can customise in Form Design view.

In many circumstances, Form view provides the best way to interact with your database.

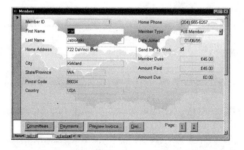

A database in Form view...

And in Datasheet view

Switching between views

You can use two methods to switch to another view.

The menu approach
Pull down the View menu and do the following:

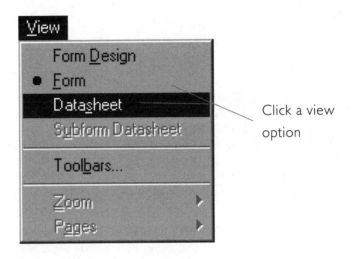

Click a view option

The Toolbar approach
The Form View toolbar displays automatically in both Form and Datasheet views.

Do the following:

Click here

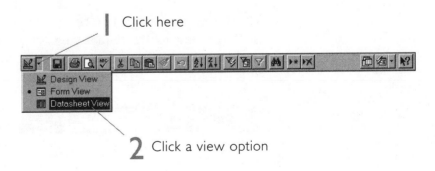

2 Click a view option

Inserting a new record

Before we can go on to discuss techniques for entering data into Access databases, we need to deal with how to create a new record, since this is a necessary prerequisite.

You can insert a new record in various ways.

The procedures for entering data are - intentionally - very similar in both Datasheet and Form views.

The menu route
In either Datasheet or Form view, pull down the Insert menu and do the following:

Click here

The toolbar route
In either Datasheet or Form view, refer to the Form View toolbar. Do the following:

Click here

The Record Gauge route
In Form view or Datasheet view, refer to the Record Gauge in the bottom left-hand corner of the screen. Do the following:

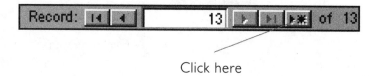

Click here

Entering data

When you've created a new record, Access places the insertion point in the first appropriate field:

This is a new record as shown in Datasheet view:

Magnified view of insertion point

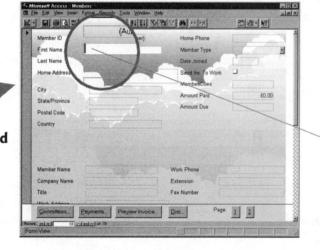

This is a new record as shown in Form view.

Magnified view of insertion point

Instead of pressing Enter, you can also press Tab.

Whichever view you're using, type in the necessary data and press Enter; Access moves the insertion point to the next field. Repeat the above procedure, as necessary. If you don't want to enter data in a field, press Enter as often as necessary until the insertion point is in a field you do want to insert data into.

Database navigation

Access makes it easy to move around in databases. The techniques for doing this are almost identical whether you're using Datasheet or Form view.

Using the Record Gauge
Press F5 to have Access place the insertion point in the Record Gauge. Then click any of the following locations to produce the specified effect:

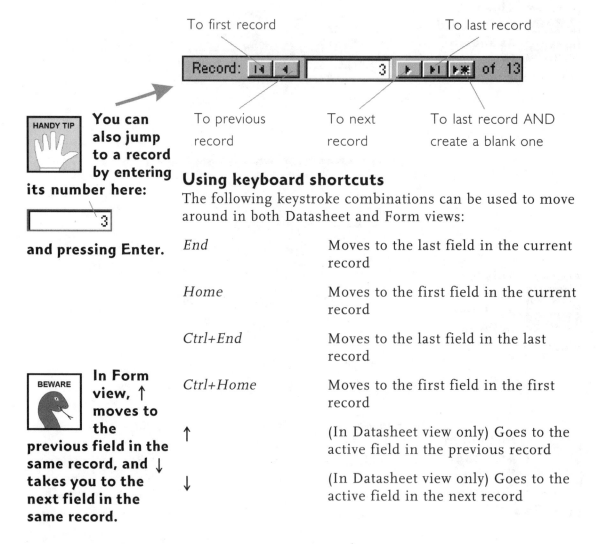

To first record

To last record

To previous record

To next record

To last record AND create a blank one

HANDY TIP

You can also jump to a record by entering its number here:

3

and pressing Enter.

Using keyboard shortcuts
The following keystroke combinations can be used to move around in both Datasheet and Form views:

End	Moves to the last field in the current record
Home	Moves to the first field in the current record
Ctrl+End	Moves to the last field in the last record
Ctrl+Home	Moves to the first field in the first record
↑	(In Datasheet view only) Goes to the active field in the previous record
↓	(In Datasheet view only) Goes to the active field in the next record

BEWARE

In Form view, ↑ moves to the previous field in the same record, and ↓ takes you to the next field in the same record.

...contd

BEWARE

In Form view, Page Up and Page Down are subject to a proviso. When the start or end of the current record has been reached, Access moves to the previous or next record, respectively.

Ctrl+ ↑	Moves to the active field in the first record
Ctrl+ ↓	Moves to the active field in the last record
Page Up	Moves up by one screen
Page Down	Moves down by one screen
F5	Places the insertion point in the Record Gauge. (See the 'Using the Record Gauge' section opposite for how to use this.)
Ctrl+Page Up	(In Datasheet view only) Moves one screen to the left
Ctrl+Page Down	(In Datasheet view only) Moves one screen to the right

BEWARE

In Form view, Ctrl+Page Up takes you to the previous record, and **Ctrl+Page Down to the next.**

Using the scroll bars

In Datasheet view, you can use the horizontal scroll bar to move through fields which aren't currently visible. The vertical scroll bar moves through records which are currently off-screen:

REMEMBER

As with all Windows 95 programs, Access only displays scroll bars if the contents of a window are too large to display in their entirety.

Vertical scroll bar

Horizontal scroll bar

In Form view, the scroll bars move you to hidden areas of the current record.

Amending data (1)

To edit existing database data, click the appropriate field in the relevant record (this applies to both Datasheet and Form views). One of two things happens now:

- if the field is empty, you can begin typing in data immediately

- if the field already contains data, Access highlights it:

First Name Karl

Simply begin typing; Access automatically overwrites the existing data.

Entering Navigation mode

Access has a special mode which lets you move around *within* fields. Navigation mode is useful (even essential) if the field contents are extensive.

When Navigation mode is active, the various keystroke combinations work as they would normally in respect of text entry in a word processor. For example, the up and down cursor keys move the insertion point up or down within the field (rather than to the previous or next fields). Home moves the insertion point to the start of the current line, rather than taking it to the start of the current record; End takes it to the finish of the current line, rather than taking it to the final field in the current record.

Magnified view of insertion
point in Navigation mode

To enter Navigation mode, click a field and press F2. To return to data entry mode, press F2 again.

Amending data (2)

Access has another, particularly useful feature which you can use when the contents of a specific field exceed its width.

Using the Zoom box

The Zoom box is, in effect, a special editing window which displays the whole of a field's contents, however extensive.

The next illustration shows the field detail section of an address field in a database form:

> Brecon House
> Fifth Floor

The address here consists of three lines, but only two display in the form. To view and/or edit the entire field, click in it. Then press Shift+F2. Now carry out the following steps:

| Type in replacement data. Or click outside the highlighted text and make any necessary revisions

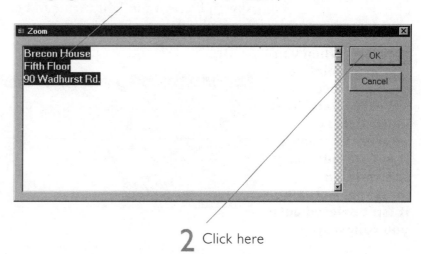

2 Click here

Deleting records (1)

It's sometimes necessary to remove unwanted records from databases. Access makes this easy, in either Datasheet or Form view.

Deleting one record

In Form view, use the techniques listed in earlier topics to move to the record you want to delete. In Datasheet view, do the following:

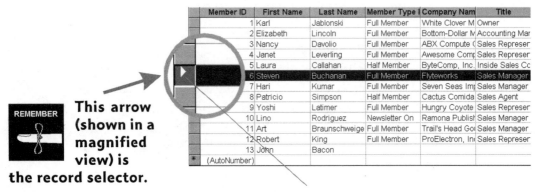

REMEMBER

This arrow (shown in a magnified view) is the record selector.

Click the appropriate entry in the Record header

Now pull down the Edit menu and click Delete Record. Access launches a warning message. Do one of the following:

REMEMBER

When you delete a record in Datasheet view, Access *appears* to remove it before launching the warning message. Actually, it isn't deleted until you follow step 1.

2 Click here to abort the deletion

Click here to delete the record

Deleting records (2)

Deleting multiple records

You have to be in Datasheet view to delete more than one record at a time. Do the following:

Click the record header entry for the 1st record you want to delete

Member ID	First Name	Last Name	Member Type	Company Nam	Title
1	Karl	Jablonski	Full Member	White Clover M	Owner
2	Elizabeth	Lincoln	Full Member	Bottom-Dollar M	Accounting Mar
3	Nancy	Davolio	Full Member	ABX Compute (	Sales Represen
4	Janet	Leverling	Full Member	Awesome Comp	Sales Represen
5	Laura	Callahan	Half Member	ByteComp, Inc.	Inside Sales Cc
6	Steven	Buchanan	Full Member	Flyteworks	Sales Manager
7	Hari	Kumar	Full Member	Seven Seas Imp	Sales Manager
8	Patricio	Simpson	Half Member	Cactus Comida	Sales Agent
9	Yoshi	Latimer	Full Member	Hungry Coyote	Sales Represen
10	Lino	Rodriguez	Newsletter On	Ramona Publisl	Sales Manager
11	Art	Braunschweige	Full Member	Trail's Head Go	Sales Manager
12	Robert	King	Full Member	ProElectron, In	Sales Represen
13	John	Bacon			
*	(AutoNumber)				

When you delete one or more records in Datasheet view, Access *appears* to remove them before launching the warning message. Actually, they aren't deleted until you follow step 1.

2 Hold down Shift and click the header entry for the final record

Now pull down the Edit menu and click Delete Record. Access launches a warning message. Do one of the following:

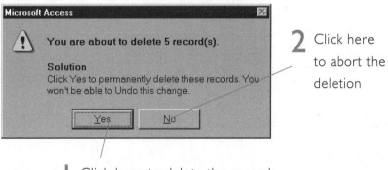

Microsoft Access

You are about to delete 5 record(s).

Solution
Click Yes to permanently delete these records. You won't be able to Undo this change.

[Yes] [No]

2 Click here to abort the deletion

Click here to delete the records

Using Undo

You can reverse many editing operations in Access. These include:

- saved changes to a record

- edits to field contents (e.g. deletions)

- all edits to the active record

The essential point to bear in mind is that you can only undo operations *if you haven't carried out any further actions of the type being undone.* For instance, if you alter and save the active record, you can only undo the amendments you've made before you edit another. If you revise the data in a field, you can only reverse this before leaving the field.

You can also use keyboard shortcuts to undo actions. For example, to undo record operations press Esc. To undo record saves and changes to field contents, press Ctrl+Z.

Undoing the last operation

Pull down the Edit menu and do the following:

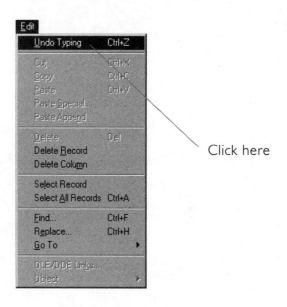

Click here

Note that the precise contents of the menu entry depend on the nature of the operation being undone.

Find operations

Access lets you search the active database for text and/or numbers. You can:

- search through all fields within every record, or limit the search to a specific field in every record

- search forwards or backwards, or through the whole database

- limit the search to exact matches (i.e. Access will only flag data which has the same upper- and lower-case make-up)

- limit the search to field sections (the beginning of fields, the whole field or any part)

Searching for data

Pull down the Edit menu and click Find. Now carry out step 1 below, then any of steps 2-5. Finally, carry out step 6 OR 7.

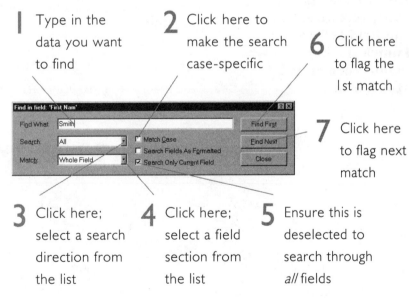

1 Type in the data you want to find

2 Click here to make the search case-specific

6 Click here to flag the 1st match

7 Click here to flag next match

3 Click here; select a search direction from the list

4 Click here; select a field section from the list

5 Ensure this is deselected to search through *all* fields

Find-and-replace operations

When you search for data you can also – if you want – have Access replace it with something else. You can:

- search through all fields within every record, or limit the search to a specific field in every record

- search forwards or backwards, or through the whole database

- limit the search to exact matches (i.e. Access will only flag data which has the same upper- and lower-case makeup)

Replacing data

Pull down the Edit menu and click Replace. Carry out steps 1-2 below, then any of 3-5. Now do *one* of the following:

- Follow step 6. When Access locates the first search target, carry out step 7 to have it replaced. Repeat as often as required

- Carry out step 8 to have every target replaced automatically

If you want to restrict the search to a specific field in every record, select the field *before* you launch the Edit menu. Then omit step 5 below.

| Type in the data you want to find

3 Click here to make the search case-specific

6 Click here to find 1st occurrence

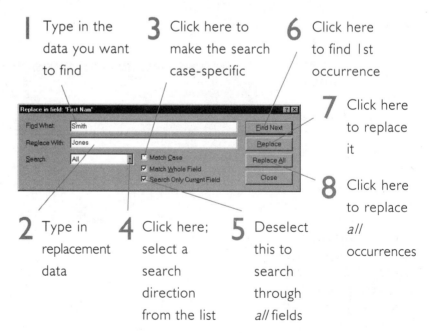

7 Click here to replace it

8 Click here to replace *all* occurrences

2 Type in replacement data

4 Click here; select a search direction from the list

5 Deselect this to search through *all* fields

Sorting data

Find operations locate specific records based on one specified criterion. However, Access lets you take this a stage further. You can have records arranged in a specific order; it calls this 'sorting'. Sorting your data often helps you find information more quickly, in both tables and forms. You can sort data in ascending order, with the following level of priority:

•   0 to 9

then

•   A to Z

You can also sort data in descending order (i.e. 9 to 0, Z to A).

Carrying out a sort

In either Datasheet or Form view, click the field on which you want to base the sort. Pull down the Records menu and click Sort, Ascending or Sort, Descending.

In Datasheet view, you can sort by more than one field (from the left). Simply select more than one column before you implement the sort.

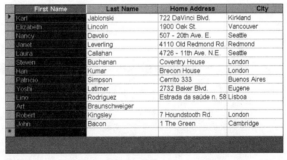

Before the sort, with the First Name field selected

To return your data to the way it was before a sort, pull down the Records menu and click Remove Filter/Sort.

After an ascending sort

Filtering data (1)

Sorting data is one way of customising the way it displays on screen. Another method you can use is 'filtering'. When you apply a filter, Access hides records which don't match the requirements ('criteria') you set.

Filtering involves:

- selecting the fields through which Access should search

- specifying the sort order (one particular advantage to filtering is that you can apply differing sort orders to the various fields)

- specifying what the fields must contain (criteria) to have their records display

- applying the filter

REMEMBER

Criteria are usually simple to use. For example, here the first field pulls in records whose First Name is John:

Setting up a filter

In Datasheet or Form view, pull down the Records menu and click Filter, Advanced Filter/Sort. Do the following:

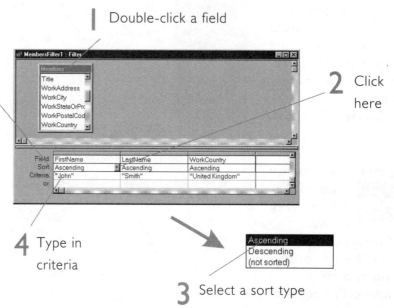

Double-click a field

2 Click here

Field: FirstName | LastName | WorkCountry
Sort: Ascending | Ascending | Ascending
Criteria: "John" | "Smith" | "United Kingdom"
or:

REMEMBER

Repeat steps 1-4 for as many fields as you want to include in the filter.

4 Type in criteria

Ascending
Descending
(not sorted)

3 Select a sort type

Filtering data (2)

Applying a filter

Once you've set up a filter, the next stage is to implement it. You can use the Filter/Sort toolbar (a special toolbar which launches automatically when you set up a filter) to do this.

Do the following:

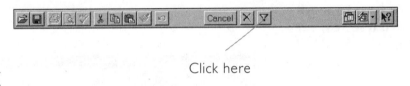

Click here

When you filter data, the effects are only temporary: the underlying table is unaffected.

The illustration below shows a filtered database:

HANDY TIP **Another way to remove a filter is to click this button:**

▽

in the Form View toolbar, *after* you've closed the Filter dialog.

Removing the filter

When you've finished with a filter, you can deactivate it.

First, close the active Filter dialog by pressing Ctrl+F4. Then pull down the Records menu and click Remove Filter/Sort.

Saving/opening filters

When you close the Filter dialog (or Access itself), details of any filter you've set up are lost. If you plan to use a filter again, however, you can save it to disk.

Access regards filters as queries. **For how to work with queries, see Chapter 6.**

Saving a filter

With the Filter dialog still open, pull down the File menu and click Save As Query. Do the following:

Saved filters appear as queries **under the Queries tab in the Database window:**

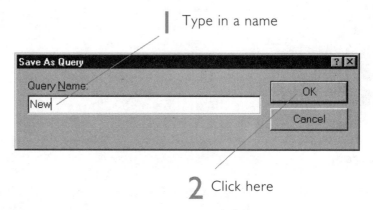

Type in a name

2 Click here

Reopening a filter

To work with a filter you've already set up, make sure the Filter dialog is open. Pull down the File menu and click Load From Query. Do the following:

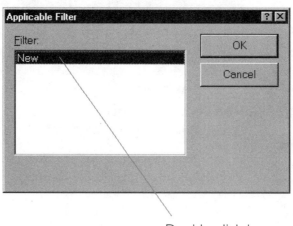

Double-click here

CHAPTER SIX

Querying databases

This chapter shows you how to retrieve highly specific information from your databases with the use of sophisticated queries. You'll learn how to create queries rapidly and easily with wizards, and apply them automatically. Then you'll create queries *manually*, for more precision. Finally, you'll save your manual query to disk, and then discover how to open and apply it.

Covers

Queries - an overview

In Chapter 5, we looked at ways to enter data into databases. However, a large part of database use consists of *extracting* information. The trick is to get precisely the information you need, in the right format. Queries represent a highly accurate and useful way of doing this.

When you set up and institute a query, you 'interrogate' the active database; the result – the 'answer' – can then be viewed on screen, or even printed. At the same time, the information which does not satisfy the criteria you set is conveniently ignored, although of course it still remains within the database. The ability to (in effect) hide information is what makes queries so indispensable.

The main types of query are:

Select queries	These extract information from tables, based on the criteria you specify. Select queries are the most frequent type, and the Access default.
Crosstab queries	These use criteria you set to summarise table data in a spreadsheet format. Crosstab queries are the most complex to use, but arguably the most useful.

Query creation

You can create queries in two ways:

•   with Query Wizards

•   manually

There are four Query Wizards; we'll examine two (the Simple Query and Crosstab Query Wizards) in this chapter.

We'll also look at manual query creation.

The Simple Query Wizard (1)

Use the Simple Query Wizard to create a Select query.

First, make sure the Database window is visible (see Chapter 3 for how to do this). Then do the following:

| Click here

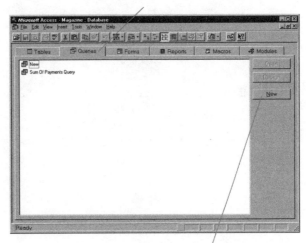

Re step 3 -
you can
run two
other
wizards here. The
Find Duplicates
Query Wizard
locates records with
duplicated field
values in any one
table; the Find
Unmatched Query
Wizard compares
tables and isolates
records which are
unrelated. To run
either of these,
simply double-click
the relevant entry
and follow the on-
screen instructions.

2 Click here

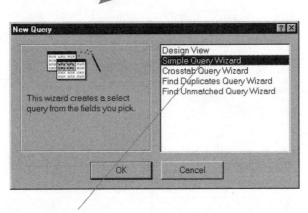

3 Double-click here

The Simple Query Wizard (2)

Now carry out the following steps:

1 Click here; select a table in the list

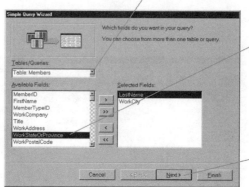

2 Double-click the field(s) you want to include in the query

HANDY TIP

Re step 1 - if you want to use fields from an additional table, click here:

Tables/Queries:

Table: Addresses

Then select a new table from the list. Finally, repeat step 2 as often as necessary. When you've specified enough fields, follow steps 3-6.

3 Click here

4 Name the query

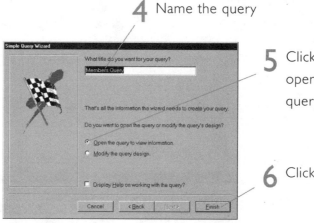

5 Click here to open the new query after step 6

6 Click here

Last Name	City
Jablonski	Seattle
Lincoln	Tsawassen
Davolio	Tacoma
Leverling	Kirkland
Callahan	
Buchanan	London
Kumar	
Simpson	Buenos Aires
Latimer	Elgin
Rodriguez	Lisboa
Braunschweige	Lander
Kingsley	London
Bacon	
Smith	

The resulting query

The Crosstab Query Wizard (1)

Crosstab queries summarise data from the fields you specify, and present it in a convenient tabular form.

First, make sure the Database window is visible (see Chapter 3 for how to do this). Then do the following:

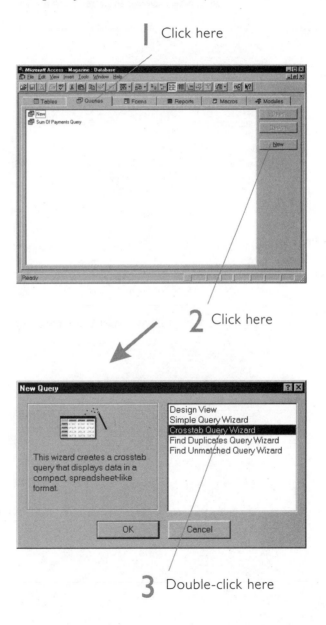

1 Click here

2 Click here

3 Double-click here

The Crosstab Query Wizard (2)

Now carry out the following steps:

In this example, we take two fields from a database created with the **MUSIC COLLECTION Wizard:**

- **Recording Title**
- **Recording Artist ID**

Then we instruct the wizard - in later dialogs - to correlate the total number of tracks in each title against the appropriate Artist ID number...

Double-click as many as 3 fields

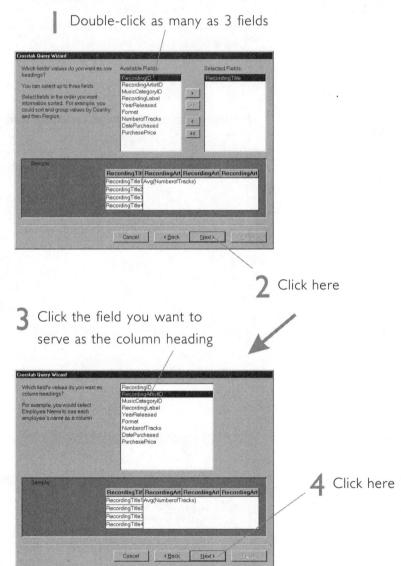

2 Click here

3 Click the field you want to serve as the column heading

4 Click here

The Crosstab Query Wizard (3)

Complete the query, as follows:

| Click a correlation field (see the Remember tip in 'The Crosstab Query Wizard (2)')

Access previews the resultant query here:

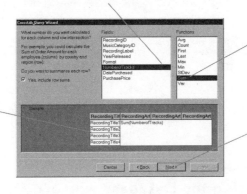

2 Click a calculation type

3 Click here

4 Name the query

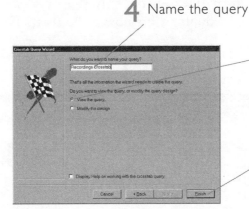

5 Click here to open the new query after step 6

6 Click here

This is the result:

Artists' ID numbers

Recording Title	Total Of NumberofTracks	1	2	3
Look Both Ways	12		12	
Meditations	6			
Noise in the Garage	10		10	
Opus 65	5	5		
Outback	10		10	
Short Circuit	7			7
Sounds Better Louder	10		10	

Individual track totals

Creating a query manually (1)

There are two ways to begin query creation manually.

Using the New Object button
Do the following:

Click here

This happens to be the Form View toolbar. However, the New Object button is in nearly every toolbar.

REMEMBER

2 Click here

Using the Database window
Alternatively, make sure the Database window is visible (see Chapter 3 for how to do this). Then do the following:

Click here

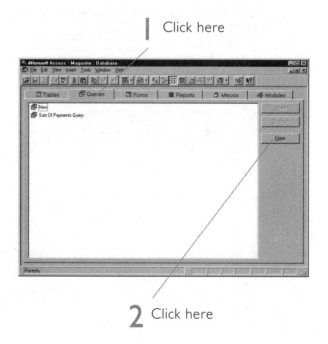

2 Click here

Creating a query manually (2)

Now carry out the following steps:

Click here

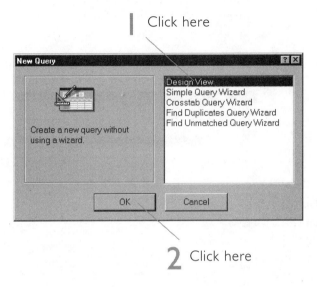

2 Click here

This is the result:

Query Design window

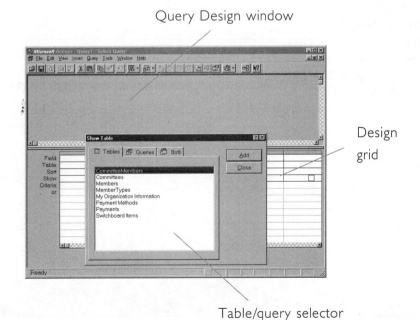

Design grid

Table/query selector

Creating a query manually (3)

The next stage is to select the tables (and/or existing queries) which contain the fields you want to insert into your query. Do the following:

Ensure this tab is active

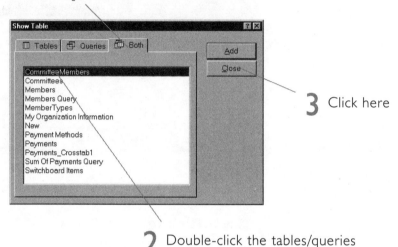

This is a magnified view of a 'join line'. Access establishes join lines when it detects that two fields have the same name and data type (and when one is a primary key). If no join lines are established, you have to rectify this – see 'Creating a query manually (4)' opposite.

3 Click here

2 Double-click the tables/queries you want to include

Access launches Field lists displaying available fields:

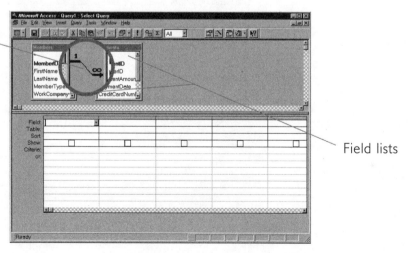

Field lists

Creating a query manually (4)

The next stage is to join tables in the Design window if:

- you have more than one Field list in the window

- the Field lists relate to tables (they probably will)

- Access hasn't already created an automatic join (see the Remember tip in the 'Creating a query manually (3)' topic for more information on this)

Do the following:

 The zoomed area shows the transformation in the mouse pointer while you create the join.

1 Click a field; drag it to its counterpart in the 2nd table

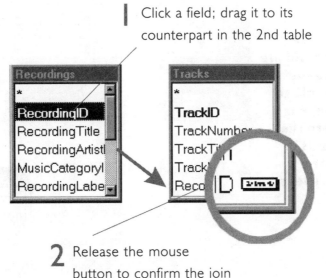

2 Release the mouse button to confirm the join

The illustration below shows the completed join:

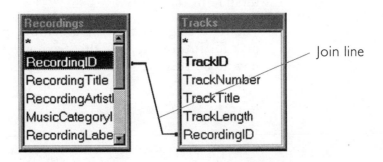

Join line

Creating a query manually (5)

Now carry out the following steps:

 Re step 1 - as you double-click *subsequent* **fields, Access inserts them in adjacent columns in the Design grid.**

 Criteria are usually simple to use. For example, here the first field pulls in records whose Recording Title is Mozart.

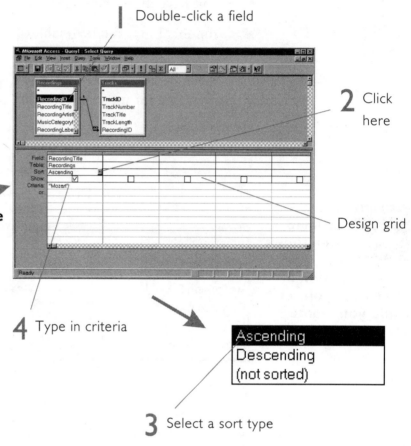

1 Double-click a field

2 Click here

Design grid

4 Type in criteria

Ascending
Descending
(not sorted)

3 Select a sort type

Repeat steps 1-4 for as many fields (using all the relevant Field lists in the Query Design window) as you want to include in the query.

The final stage in creating a manual query is to save it to disk for future use. See the 'Saving your query' topic for how to do this.

Saving your query

Manually generated queries need to be saved to disk for later use.

You can also use the procedures outlined in this topic to save existing queries under a new name.

Saving a query

With the Query Design window still open, pull down the File menu and do the following:

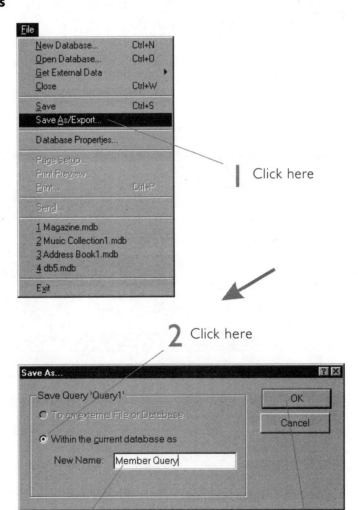

Click here

2 Click here

3 Name the query

4 Click here

Applying/opening queries

HANDY TIP

You can also apply a query directly from within the Query Design window. Simply pull down the Query menu and click Run.

When you open a query you've previously saved to disk, Access applies it to your data. (When you create a new query with a wizard, by default Access opens it automatically – see earlier topics for more information on this. However, with a manually generated query you must open it yourself.)

Opening a query

First, ensure the Database window is visible (for how to do this, see 'The Database window' topic in Chapter 3). Now do the following:

Activate the Queries tab

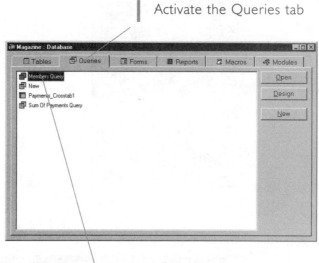

2 Double-click the query you want to open

Closing down a query

In any open query, do the following:

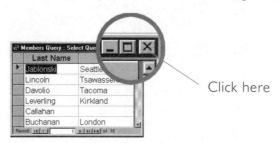

Click here

CHAPTER SEVEN

Creating reports

This chapter shows you how to view your data as reports. You'll learn how to create straightforward reports rapidly and easily with AutoReports. You'll also build more complex reports with the Report Wizard. Then you'll create reports *manually*, for more precision, and you'll discover how to customise the way report components display. Finally, you'll save your manually generated report to disk, and then discover how to view it.

Covers

Reports - an overview

In Chapter 4, we looked at the creation and use of database forms. Forms allow you to enter data in a user-friendly way. Reports, on the other hand, have a similar effect on the way you view (and print) data. In fact, when you create and view a report, you have:

- more control over the layout

- the ability to customise the printed output (see Chapter 9 for more information on printing reports)

Before you set up and institute a report, you should do the following:

HANDY TIP

Reports can be based on either tables or queries; or instances of both.

- examine your database, taking account of the current tables, forms and queries

- be clear in your own mind which components of your database represent data, and make sure you've entered all the data you want reports to display

- if you want to enter data *as well as* view it, use a form (you can't enter information into reports)

- if you've created previous reports (or if you've used a wizard to create a database and reports have been created automatically in the process, as is normally the case), review them with a view to highlighting areas which need improving.

Report creation

You can create reports in two ways:

- with Report Wizards/AutoReports

- manually

There are three main Report Wizards/AutoReports; we'll examine these in later topics.

We'll also look at manual report creation.

Report Wizards

The three principal wizards are:

Columnar AutoReport   Automatically creates a quick, simple report for the selected table in a single column

Tabular AutoReport   Automatically creates a quick, simple report for the selected table in a table format

Report Wizard   Provides full control over which tables and fields are included, and extensive customisation

The AutoReports are an especially quick and convenient way to create reports. Use the Report Wizard when you need greater precision.

Members

MemberID	1
FirstName	Karl
LastName	Jablonski
MemberTypeID	1
WorkCompany	White Clover Markets
Title	Owner
WorkAddress	305 - 14th Ave. S.
WorkCity	Seattle
WorkStateOrProvi	WA
WorkPostalCode	98128
WorkCountry	USA
WorkPhone	(206) 555-4112
Extension	

Columnar
AutoReport

MemberID	FirstName	LastName	erTypeID	WorkComp	Title	WorkAddress
1	Karl	Jablonski	1	White Clover M	Owner	305 - 14th Ave. S.
2	Elizabeth	Lincoln	1	Bottom-Dollar	Accounting Ma	23 Tsawassen Blvd.
3	Nancy	Davolio	1	AEX Compute	Sales Represent	908 W. Capital Way
4	Janet	Leverling	1	Awesome Com	Sales Represent	722 Moss Bay Blvd.
5	Laura	Callahan	2	ByteComp, Inc.	Inside Sales Co	
6	Steven	Buchanan	1	Flyteworks	Sales Manager	14 Garrett Hill
7	Hari	Kumar	1	Seven Seas Imp	Sales Manager	
8	Patricio	Simpson	2	Cactus Comidas	Sales Agent	Ing. Gustavo Moncal
9	Yoshi	Latimer	1	Hungry Coyote	Sales Represent	City Center Plaza
10	Lino	Rodriguez	3	Ramona Publis	Sales Manager	Jardim das rosas n. 3
11	Art	Braunschweiger	1	Trail's Head Go	Sales Manager	P.O. Box 555
12	Robert	Kingsley	1	ProElectron, Inc	Sales Represent	Edgeham Hollow
13	John	Bacon				

Tabular
AutoReport

Creating AutoReport reports

First, make sure the Database window is visible (see Chapter 3 for how to do this). Now carry out the following steps:

Ensure the Reports tab is active

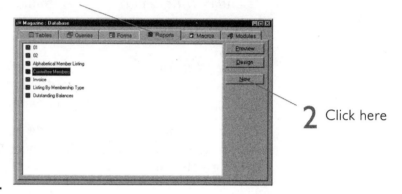

2 Click here

Re step 5 - Access provides an extra Report Wizard: the Label Wizard. This creates reports which produce highly customisable labels in various formats. To run the Label Wizard, simply double-click its name in the New Report dialog box and follow the on-screen instructions.

5 Click an AutoReport option

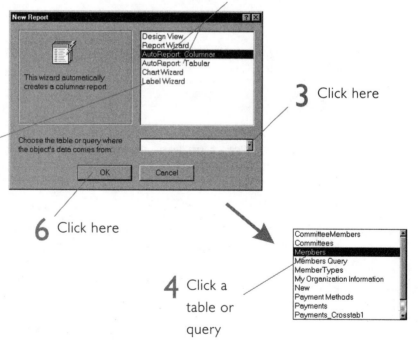

3 Click here

6 Click here

4 Click a table or query

Using the Report Wizard (1)

First, make sure the Database window is visible (see Chapter 3 for how to do this). Now carry out the following steps:

1 | Ensure the Reports tab is active

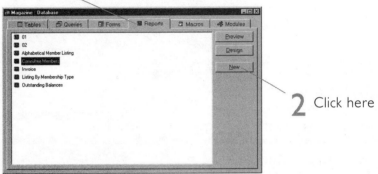

2 Click here

5 Click here

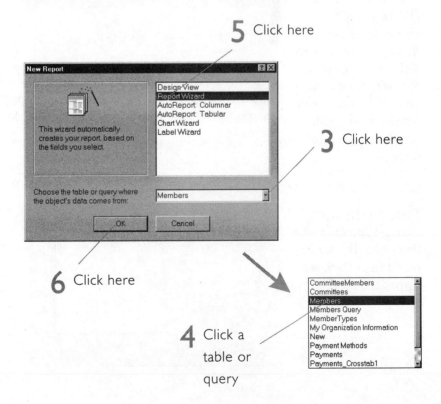

3 Click here

6 Click here

4 Click a table or query

Using the Report Wizard (2)

Now carry out the following steps:

Double-click the field(s) you want to include

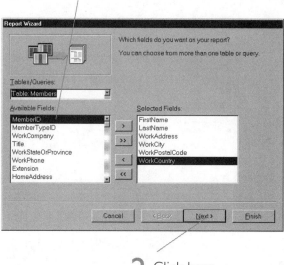

HANDY TIP

Re step 1 - when you carried out steps 3 & 4 earlier in the 'Using the Report Wizard (1)' topic, you selected a table or query on which to base your new report. If you want to use fields from an *additional* **table and/or query, click here:**

Tables/Queries:

| Table: Addresses |

Then make a selection from the list. Finally, carry out steps 2-4, as appropriate.

2 Click here

In the next dialog, if any of the fields can be grouped under a convenient heading (this makes reports easier to follow), carry out steps 3 and 4 below (if not, simply follow step 4):

3 Double-click the heading field

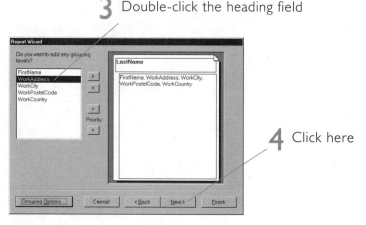

4 Click here

Using the Report Wizard (3)

 If you followed steps 3 AND 4 in 'Using the Report Wizard (2)', you now allocate sort fields for 'detail records' (those organised under group headings); if you defined no headings, you sort *all* records here.

In the next dialog you can select up to four sort fields as a basis for ordering records. Carry out steps 1-3 below (to allocate more than one sort field, repeat steps 1-2 for fields below the first, THEN follow 3). Finally, follow steps 4-6.

I Click here

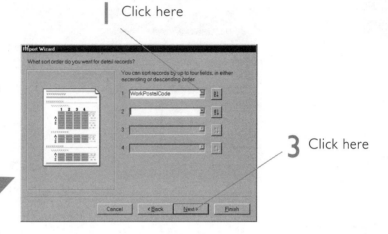

3 Click here

 Click the button to the right of each sort field:

 Ascending

 Descending

to toggle between Ascending or Descending sorts.

2 Click a field

4 Choose a report layout

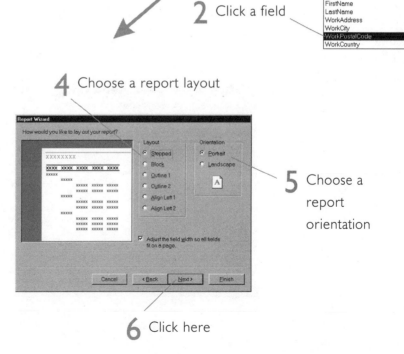

5 Choose a report orientation

6 Click here

Using the Report Wizard (4)

Now carry out the following steps:

Select a report style

Access previews report styles here:

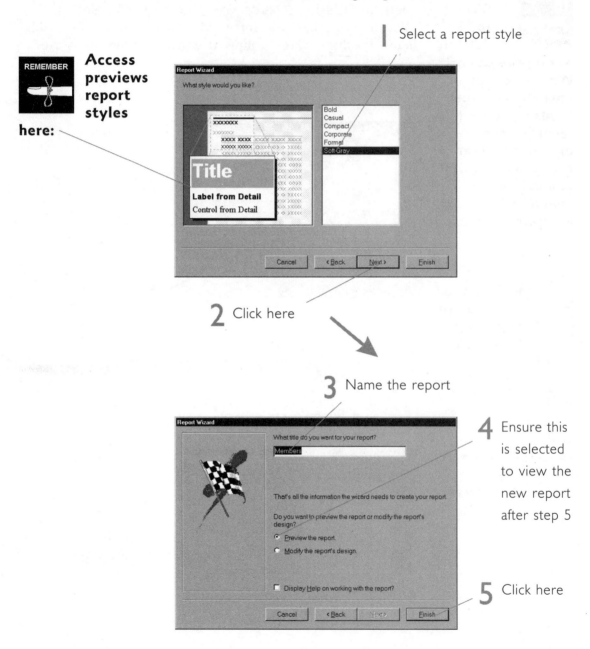

2 Click here

3 Name the report

4 Ensure this is selected to view the new report after step 5

5 Click here

Creating reports manually (1)

There are two ways to begin report creation manually.

Using the New Object button
Do the following:

Click here

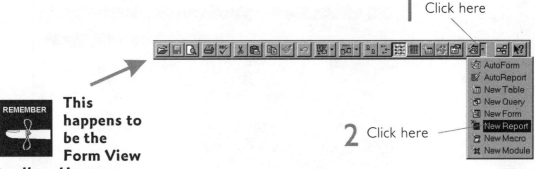

2 Click here

REMEMBER **This happens to be the Form View toolbar. However, the New Object button is in nearly every toolbar.**

Using the Database window
Alternatively, make sure the Database window is visible (see Chapter 3 for how to do this). Then do the following:

Ensure the Reports tab is active

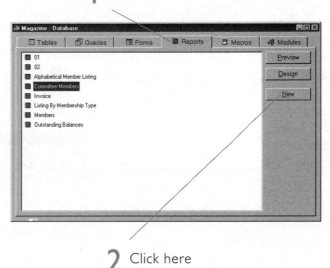

2 Click here

Creating reports manually (2)

Now carry out the following steps:

Click here

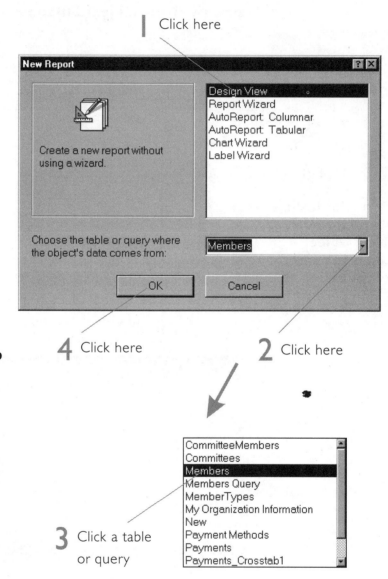

4 Click here

2 Click here

After step 4, Access creates a blank report. See the 'Amending report design' topics later (et al) for how to customise it.

3 Click a table or query

Report design - an overview

HANDY TIP **If you want to, you can also opt to** *redesign* **reports created with the various wizards.**

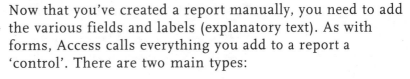

Now that you've created a report manually, you need to add the various fields and labels (explanatory text). As with forms, Access calls everything you add to a report a 'control'. There are two main types:

* bound

* unbound

Bound controls pull in data from fields in an underlying database table or query. For instance, if a field in a table contains Address information, the relevant control will return location data for the currently active record.

HANDY TIP **To see what your work looks like at any stage in the report design process, pull down the View menu and click Print Preview. To continue your design work, pull down the same menu and click Report Design.**

Unbound controls, on the other hand, contain supplementary text (e.g. instructions to the database user) or graphics components (e.g. lines); they aren't connected to table fields.

The illustration below shows an excerpt from a previewed report:

Labels

Alphabetical Member Listing

Member Name	Member Type	Work Phone
B		
John Bacon		
Art Braunschweiger	Full Member	(307) 555-4680
Steven Buchanan	Full Member	(71) 555-4848

Bound fields

Amending report design (1)

There are two ways to begin customising a report's design.

If the report is already open
Pull down the View menu and do the following:

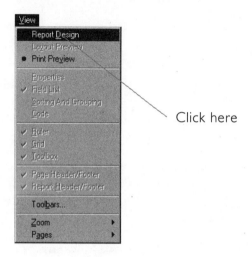

Click here

If the report isn't already open
Go to the Database window (see 'The Database window' topic in Chapter 3 for how to do this) and do the following:

Ensure the Reports tab is active

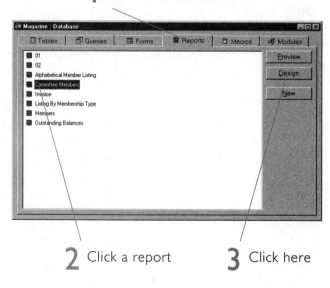

2 Click a report   **3** Click here

Amending report design (2)

If you've just created a manual report, you'll already be in Report Design view.

Access now launches the report in Report Design view. This is the basis for adding and customising fields. The following components are especially important:

- the Detail pane

- the Toolbox

- the Field List

If the Field List isn't currently visible, pull down the View menu and click Field List.

Detail pane

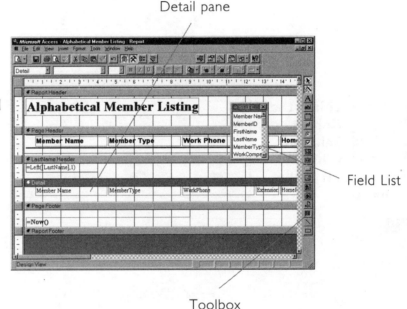

Field List

Toolbox

You can resize the Detail pane.
Move the mouse pointer over a side or corner (the pointer changes to a 4-pronged arrow). Click and drag appropriately. Release the button to confirm the operation.

The Detail pane represents the current body of your report. Here, you create and design the necessary fields.

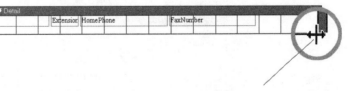

Magnified view of resizing cursor

AutoFormat

You can apply a series of pre-defined formats to overall report design. Use AutoFormat to impose:

- a background

- a preset control font

- a preset control border

Using AutoFormat
Do the following to select the entire report:

Click here

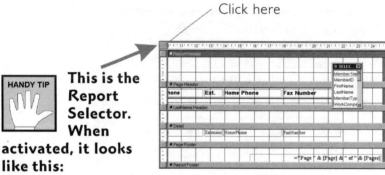

HANDY TIP

This is the Report Selector. When activated, it looks like this:

Now pull down the Format menu and click AutoFormat. Do the following:

Double-click a style

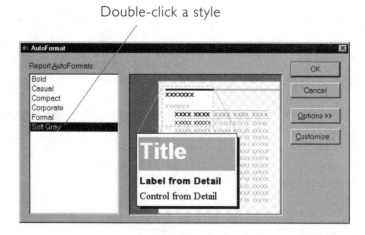

Adding labels (1)

It's useful to add descriptive labels to reports. Report areas you can add labels to include:

Unlike forms, Access reports automatically display header and footer areas.

- the report header or footer

- the Detail pane

First, refer to the Report toolbox and do the following:

Click here

Move the pointer to the appropriate location in the header/footer or Detail pane. Hold down the left mouse button and drag to define the label area:

Label area

This magnified view shows how the cursor changes when you're defining a label:

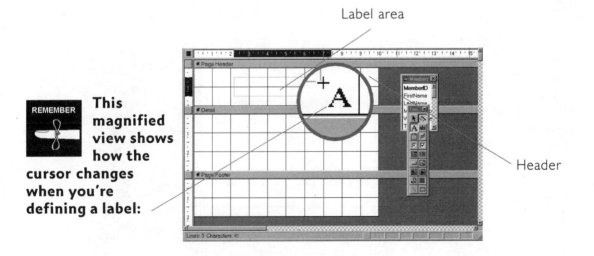

Header

Release the mouse button to complete the label.

Adding labels (2)

So far, your label will look something like this:

Label

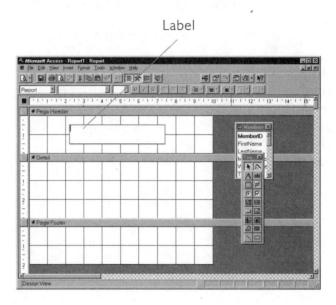

The next stage is to type in the label text. When you've finished, press Enter.

HANDY TIP

You'll probably need to reformat most labels after you've created them. See the various 'Reformatting labels and fields' topics later for how to do this.

The inserted (but not yet reformatted) label

Adding fields

Once you've inserted the necessary labels, the next stage is to insert the required fields. This is a simple process which involves a drag-and-drop technique.

In Report Design view, make sure the Field List is visible. (If it isn't, pull down the View menu and click Field List.) Then do the following:

2 Drag it to the appropriate location in the report

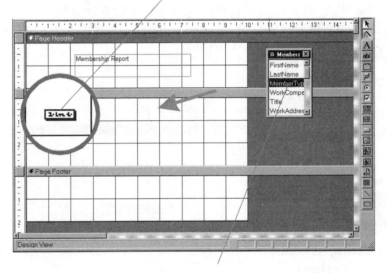

Click a field

Fields in reports consist of two parts:

- **the field name:**

| Member Type |

- **the field detail:**

| MemberTypeID ▾ |

Release the mouse button to insert the new field:

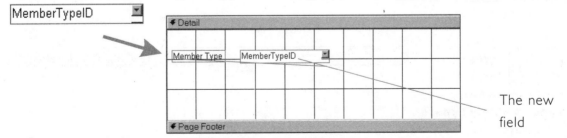

The new field

Reformatting labels and fields (1)

Once you've inserted a new label or field, you can:

You can select multiple controls by holding down Shift as you click them.

- apply a new typeface

- apply a new type size

- align the contents

- apply foreground and/or background colours

- specify a border width and/or colour

If you want to reformat the field name *as well as* the field detail, don't forget to select it as well.

Applying a new typeface
First, select the control(s) you want to amend. Then do the following:

Formatting operations on controls use the Formatting (Form/ Report Design) toolbar; it's automatically present in Report Design view.

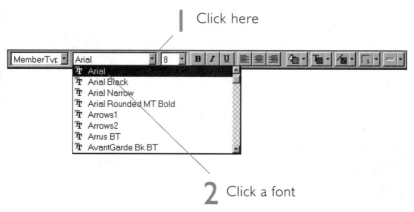

Click here

2 Click a font

Applying a new type size
First, select the control(s) you want to amend. Then do the following:

For greater precision, simply type in a new type size here:
Then press Return.

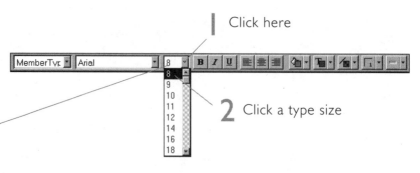

Click here

2 Click a type size

Reformatting labels and fields (2)

Aligning label and field contents

First, click the control you want to amend. (If you want to select more than one, hold down Shift at the same time.) Then carry out any of the following:

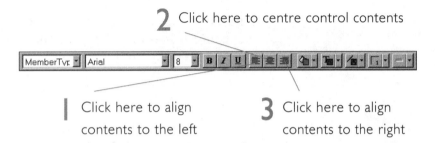

2 Click here to centre control contents

| Click here to align contents to the left

3 Click here to align contents to the right

Colouring foregrounds and backgrounds

First, click the control you want to amend. (If you want to select more than one, hold down Shift at the same time.) Then follow steps 1 AND 2 to apply a background colour, or 3 AND 4 to apply a foreground colour:

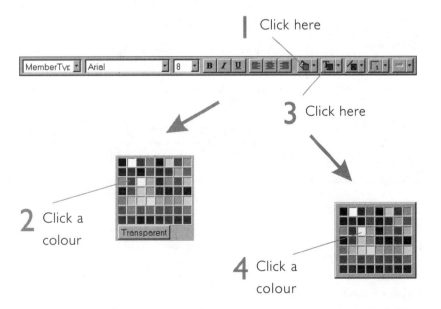

| Click here

3 Click here

2 Click a colour

4 Click a colour

Reformatting labels and fields (3)

Specifying a border width

You can apply a small number of pre-defined line widths to controls. Note, however, that you can only apply the appropriate border to *all four sides* of a control: you can't specify which edges you border.

First, click the control you want to amend. (If you want to select more than one, hold down Shift at the same time.) Then do the following:

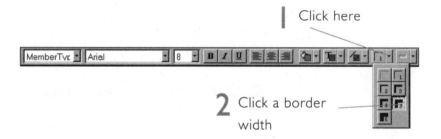

Click here

2 Click a border width

Specifying a border colour

First, click the control you want to amend. (If you want to select more than one, hold down Shift at the same time.)

Then do the following:

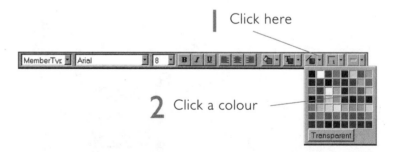

Click here

2 Click a colour

Saving your report

Manually generated reports need to be saved to disk for later use.

You can also use the procedures outlined in this topic to save existing reports under a new name.

Saving a report
Within Report Design view, pull down the File menu and do the following:

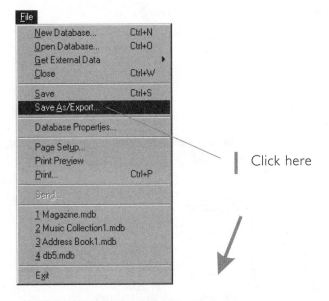

Click here

2 Click here

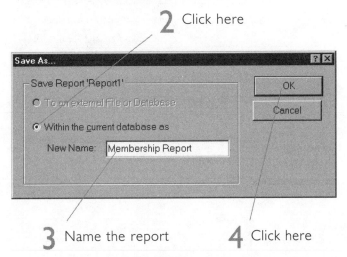

3 Name the report   4 Click here

Opening reports

When you open a report you've previously saved to disk, Access displays it in Print Preview mode. (When you create a new report with a wizard, by default Access opens it automatically – see earlier topics for more information on this. However, with a manual report you must open it yourself when you want to view it.)

You can't edit reports in Print Preview mode: you can only inspect them.

Opening a report

First, ensure the Database window is visible (for how to do this, see 'The Database window' topic in Chapter 3). Now do the following:

Activate the Reports tab

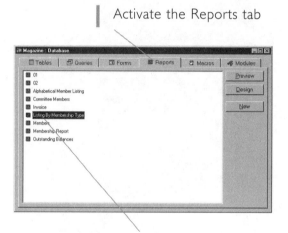

2 Double-click the report you want to view

Closing down a report

Do the following:

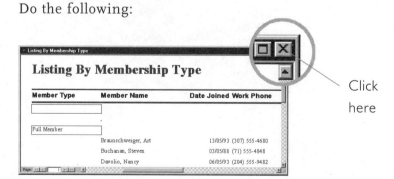

Click here

CHAPTER EIGHT

Creating graphs

This chapter shows you how to view your data graphically, as a chart. You'll learn to create charts either as separate forms or reports in their own right, or as part of existing forms/reports. You'll learn how to specify the chart type, either during the process of creation or subsequently. You'll also discover how to launch Microsoft Graph, to modify the underlying data or format of your graphs in a variety of ways.

Covers

Graphs - an overview

Graphs give your data visual impact, and make it more assimilable. They also:

- reveal hidden relationships between data

- make trends much more apparent

In one sense, graphs are similar to forms and reports: they let you view your data in a highly specific – and useful – fashion.

Graph creation

You create graphs in Access with the help of the Graph Wizard. You can use this wizard in two ways:

- when you create a special form or report from scratch

- from within existing forms or reports, in Form Design or Report Design modes

The first method is the easiest and quickest way to create a new graph. When you create a graph in this way, Access builds a new form or report with a single graph in it.

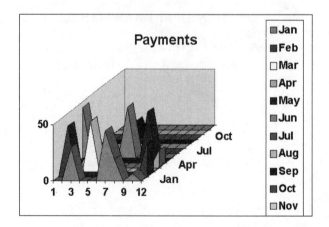

A new graph, excerpted from a form

When you use the second method, however, the result is identical with one exception: you can choose to link the graph to fields in the form/report.

Creating a graph from scratch (1)

First, ensure the Database window is visible (for how to do this, see Chapter 3). Then carry out the following steps:

Activate either of these tabs

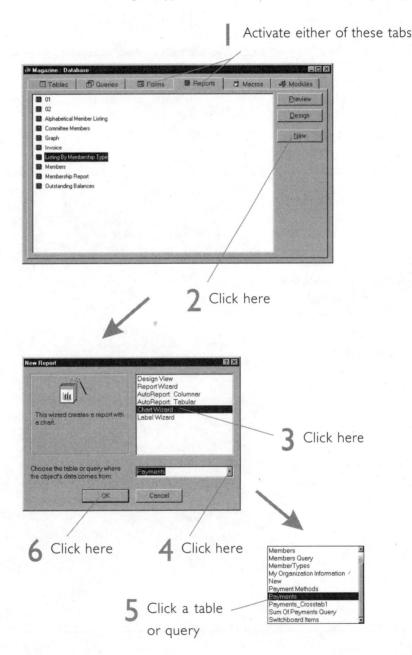

2 Click here

3 Click here

6 Click here

4 Click here

5 Click a table
or query

Creating a graph from scratch (2)

Now carry out the following steps:

Double-click the fields you want to include

At least one of the fields you select must contain numerical data (e.g. - as here - currency information).

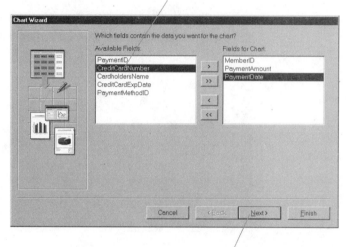

Access provides a potted description of each chart format here:

2 Click here

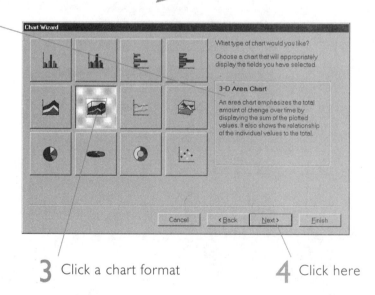

3 Click a chart format   4 Click here

Creating a graph from scratch (3)

In the next dialog, Access displays the selected fields as buttons. It makes certain assumptions about which axes the fields should occupy, and displays a brief illustration of the result on the left of the dialog. If you want to change these assumptions, carry out steps 1-2 below, then follow step 3. If you don't, simply follow step 3:

| Click and hold on a field button...

HANDY TIP

Re step 2 – when you drag the field button, the cursor changes - see the magnified section in the dialog.

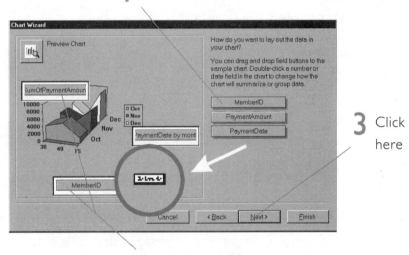

3 Click here

2 Drag it to an axis box

Previewing your chart

Before you proceed, you can inspect how your chart looks. Click the Preview Chart button: in the top left-hand corner of the above dialog. This is the result:

HANDY TIP

To close the Preview window and continue with the Chart Wizard, press Esc. Follow step 3 above to move on to the next stage...

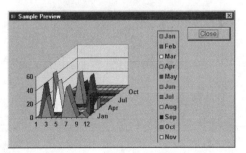

Creating a graph from scratch (4)

Carry out the final steps below:

The Chart Wizard assumes you want a 'legend' (text which links chart colours with the data they represent) included in the chart. If you don't, click here *before* step 3:

Name the chart

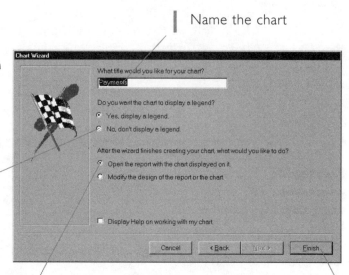

2 Ensure this is selected to have Access launch the chart after step 3

3 Click here

This is the final result (in this instance, Access has opened the report which contains the new chart):

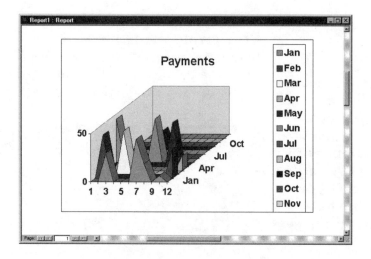

Creating an in-line graph (1)

The example discussed in this and subsequent topics shows the addition of a graph to an existing form; the procedure is essentially the same for a report.

You can also run the Graph Wizard from within an existing form or report; however, the launch procedure is different.

First, open the relevant form or report (for how to do this, see the appropriate topics in Chapters 4 and 7 respectively). Then switch to Form Design or Report Design views by pulling down the View menu and clicking Form Design or Report Design. Finally, pull down the Insert menu and do the following:

Click here

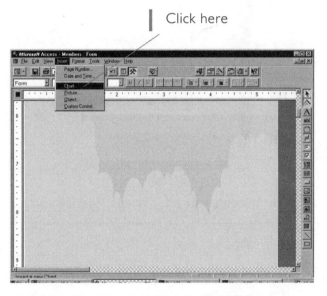

The mouse cursor changes:

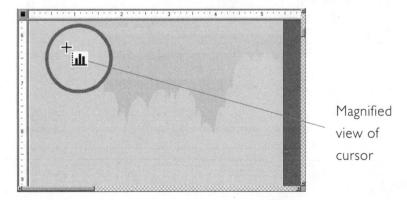

Magnified view of cursor

Creating an in-line graph (2)

Position the transformed cursor at the point where you
want the chart to begin. Press and hold down the left
mouse button; drag to define the chart area:

Defined chart area

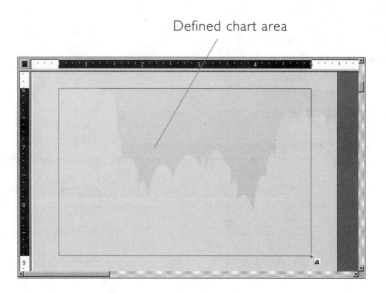

When you release the mouse button, the dialog below
launches. Carry out the following steps:

2 Click a table or query

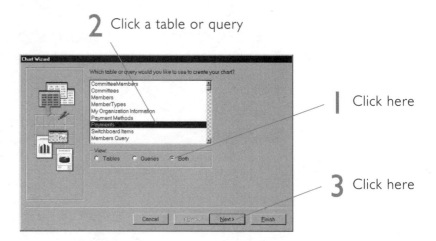

Click here

3 Click here

Creating an in-line graph (3)

Complete the following steps:

1 Double-click the field(s) you want to include

Chart Wizard

Which fields contain the data you want for the chart?

Available Fields:

PaymentID
CreditCardNumber
CardholdersName
CreditCardExpDate
PaymentMethodID

Fields for Chart:

MemberID
PaymentAmount
PaymentDate

[>] [>>] [<] [<<]

Cancel   < Back   Next >   Finish

2 Click here

3 Click a chart format

Chart Wizard

What type of chart would you like?

Choose a chart that will appropriately display the fields you have selected.

3-D Column Chart

A 3-D perspective column chart compares data points along two axes, showing variation over a period of time or illustrates comparisons among items.

Cancel   < Back   Next >   Finish

REMEMBER **Access provides a potted description of each chart format here:**

4 Click here

Creating an in-line graph (4)

Now, Access displays the selected fields as buttons and makes certain assumptions about which axes the fields should occupy. If you want to change these assumptions, carry out steps 1-2 below, then follow step 3. If you don't, simply follow step 3:

| Click and hold on a field button...

HANDY TIP

Re step 2 - when you drag the field button, the cursor changes - see the magnified section in the dialog.

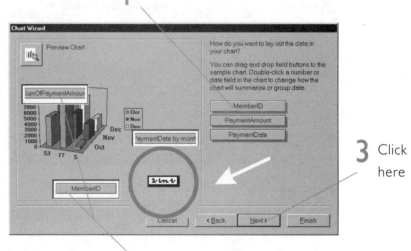

3 Click here

2 Drag it to an axis box

If you want to link the data in your graph with fields in the underlying form or report, do the following:

HANDY TIP

If you don't want to link any fields, simply carry out step 6.

4 Click here; select a field in the list

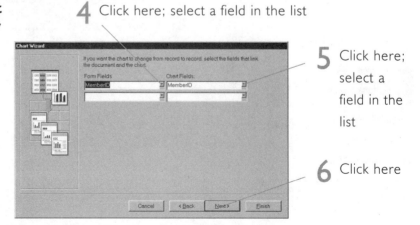

5 Click here; select a field in the list

6 Click here

Creating an in-line graph (5)

Carry out the final steps below:

The Chart Wizard assumes you want a 'legend' (text which links chart colours with the data they represent) included in the chart. If you don't, click here *before* step 2:

| Name the chart

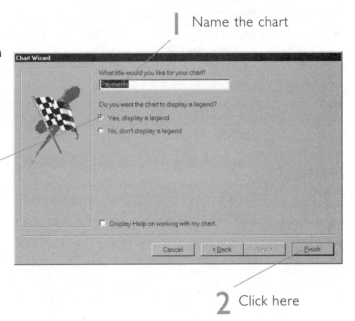

2 Click here

This is the final result (in this instance, Access has inserted the new chart into the original form):

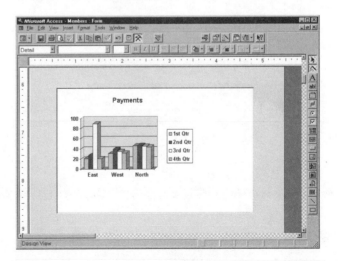

Amending graphs (1)

However you use the Graph Wizard (either in the creation of a new form/report or from within an existing form/report), what actually happens is that Access launches a separate program – Microsoft Graph – behind the scenes. With the use of a kind of sleight of hand, Microsoft Graph creates the chart and inserts it seamlessly into your form or report.

To modify charts, however, you have to make Microsoft Graph visible.

Launching Microsoft Graph (1)

This is a two-stage process. The first stage is to launch (in Design view) the form or report which contains the chart you want to alter.

Make sure the Database window is visible (for how to do this, see Chapter 3). Then do the following:

Activate either of these tabs

2 Click the holding form or report

3 Click here

Amending graphs (2)

Launching Microsoft Graph (2)

In the second stage, do the following:

 Here, the chart is shown after a _single_ click, for illustration purposes.

Double-click anywhere in the chart area

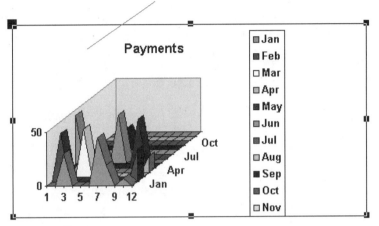

This is the result:

Datasheet window

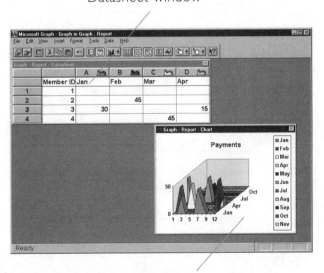

Microsoft Graph

Chart window

Amending graphs (3)

Microsoft Graph consists of two components:

- the Datasheet window

- the Chart window

You can use the Datasheet window to enter or amend data; it works as a cut-down version of an Access table (see the relevant topics in Chapter 3 for how to use it).

You can use the Chart window to:

Amend the chart type Pull down the Format menu and click Chart Type. Select a new 2-D or 3-D type in the dialog and click OK to apply it.

Apply a preset format Pull down the Format menu and click AutoFormat. Select a Gallery – chart type – and then a sub-type. Click OK to apply it.

Change the typeface and/or type size for legends

Select the text by clicking it. Pull down the Format menu and click Font. In the dialog, click a new font or size. Click OK to apply your changes.

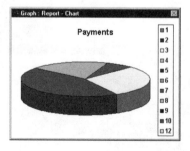

The original chart with its chart type changed to 3-D Pie

When you've finished working in Microsoft Graph, pull down the File menu and click Exit & Return to Graph: Report. You're returned to Access (the original chart is automatically updated in line with your work).

CHAPTER NINE

Printing your data

This chapter shows you how to print out your data. Before you do this, however, you'll learn how to ensure that the overall page layout is correct. You'll discover how to revise margin settings, allocate a page size/orientation and – in the case of forms and reports – specify column dimensions. You'll go on to preview your work, using the Access Print Preview window, before finally customising print settings and printing your work.

Covers

Printing – an overview

Access handles printing in broadly the same way, irrespective of whether you're printing tables, forms, reports or queries.

In spite of this, however, there are differences:

• tables and queries have fewer incidental criteria (principally, margins and page size) you can set before you begin a print-run

• with forms and reports, you can set a variety of additional layout and page setup criteria (principally relating to multi-column documents) before you begin printing

In spite of these discrepancies, you can always preview your work before you commit yourself to printing it. This is advisable because:

• the Access Print Preview screen provides a fully WYSIWYG (What You See Is What You Get) representation of what your data will look like when printed

• Access data (especially in tables) frequently spreads across more than one page; Print Preview gives you a bird's-eye view of this process in operation

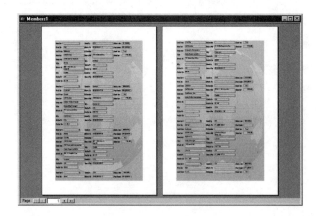

A form
in Print
Preview

Page Setup issues (1)

If you intend to print tables, queries, forms or reports, you need to ensure that the correct page setup/layout criteria are in force before you do so.

First, ensure the Database window is open (for how to do this, refer to Chapter 3). Carry out the following steps:

Activate one of these tabs

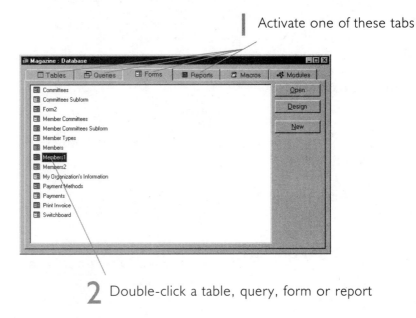

2 Double-click a table, query, form or report

The selected database component is opened. Now pull down the File menu and do the following:

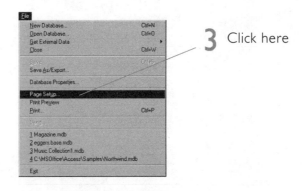

3 Click here

Page Setup issues (2)

Setting margin sizes

Follow the procedures on page 145 then do the following:

Ensure this tab is active

 In tables, this option is Print Headings. Deselect it if you don't want column headings to print.

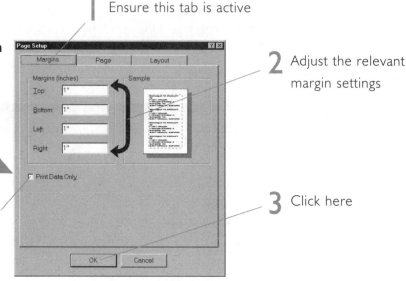

2 Adjust the relevant margin settings

3 Click here

 Click here: to have Access ignore gridlines, borders and labels when you begin the print-run.

Setting page size/orientation

Carry out step 1 below, then 2 and/or 3. Then follow step 4:

Activate this tab

 Re step 2 – see the following for details of orientation types:

 Portrait

 Landscape

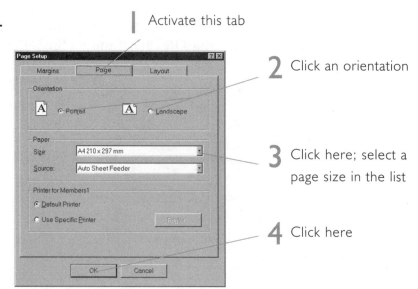

2 Click an orientation

3 Click here; select a page size in the list

4 Click here

Page Setup issues (3)

Specifying column layouts

In forms or reports, you can determine:

- how many columns data prints in

- the gap between rows

- the inter-column spacing

- the column width and/or height

- the order in which Access prints fields within records

Follow the procedure on page 145 then carry out step 1 below. Follow steps 2-5, as appropriate, then step 6:

 Click the relevant option here to determine print direction:

 Down, then Across

 Across, then Down

Finally, follow step 6.

2 Type in the no. of columns

1 Activate this tab

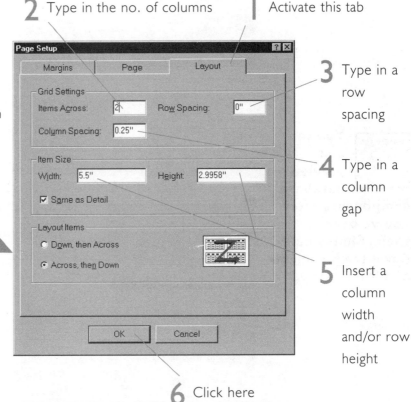

3 Type in a row spacing

4 Type in a column gap

5 Insert a column width and/or row height

6 Click here

Launching Print Preview

You can preview any database component before printing it.

First, launch the Database window (see Chapter 3 for how to do this). Then carry out the following steps.

Activate one of these tabs

2 Click the table, query, form or report you want to preview

HANDY TIP **You can also preview database components after you've opened them. Simply pull down the File menu and follow step 3:**

Now pull down the File menu and do the following:

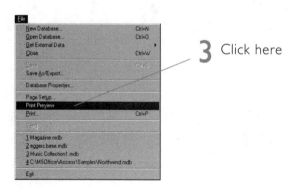

3 Click here

Using Print Preview (1)

When you opt to preview a database component, Access launches a special Print Preview window showing how the component will look when printed:

Print Preview toolbar

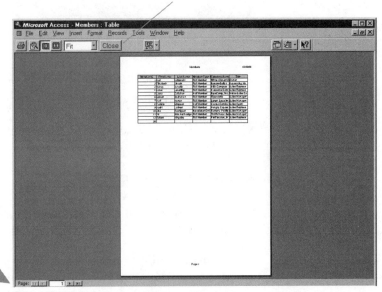

REMEMBER

These are the Print Preview navigation controls. See over for how to use them.

The Print Preview window has its own dedicated toolbar (see above). You can use this to:

- zoom in or out (there are two methods)

- apply a preset Zoom percentage (e.g. 150%, 200%)

- specify the view spread (1 or 2 pages)

- initiate printing immediately

You can also use the navigation controls in the bottom left-hand corner of the Print Preview window to (among other things) move to a precise page instantly.

Using Print Preview (2)

Zooming in and out (1)

Do the following:

Click here

to alternate between:

- Full Page view (where the whole page is visible in the Print Preview window)

- whichever Zoom level was previously set (see the 'Using Print Preview (3)' topic)

Zooming in and out (2)

You can also use a variation on the above technique to select which area of the database component you want to zoom in on.

Carry out the above procedure, then position the mouse pointer over the section of the Print Preview window you want to magnify – the cursor becomes a magnifying glass:

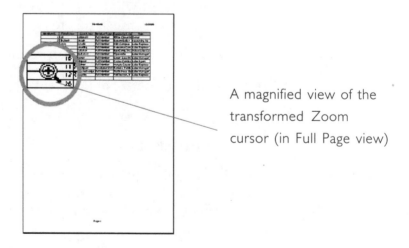

A magnified view of the transformed Zoom cursor (in Full Page view)

Left-click once to zoom in; click again to revert to Full Page view.

Using Print Preview (3)

Applying a preset Zoom percentage

Do the following:

 HANDY TIP **To specify your own Zoom %, instead of** following step 2, type in a % here: then press Enter.

| Click here

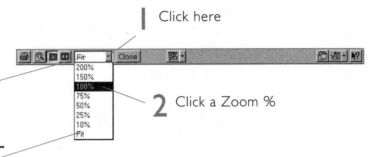

2 Click a Zoom %

200%
150%
100%
75%
50%
25%
10%
Fit

 HANDY TIP **Re step 2 – click Fit to have Access** choose a Zoom level which displays your table, query, form or report optimally, according to the size of the window.

Specifying the view spread

Do the following:

Click here to view a single page

Click here to view two pages

A one-page spread

A two-page spread

Using Print Preview (4)

Initiating a print-run

If you know that the relevant print criteria are correctly set (see the 'Printing your data' topics next for how to set these), you can use the Print Preview toolbar to have Access start printing *immediately*, without launching the Print dialog.

Do the following:

Click here

Using the navigation controls

You can use the navigation controls in the bottom left-hand corner of the Print Preview window to jump to:

- a specific page

- the previous page

- the next page

- the first page

- the last page

Click where indicated below (or to move to a specific page, enter the page number):

REMEMBER

To close the Print Preview window, simply press Esc. Or click:

Close

in the Print Preview toolbar.

To the
1st page

Type in a page no.
and press Enter

To the
last page

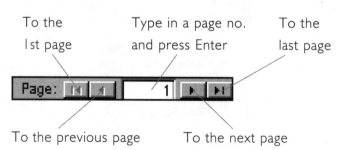

Page: |◄| |◄| 1 |►| |►|

To the previous page   To the next page

Printing your data (1)

Printing is a two-stage process.

Preparing to print

First, preview the database component you want to print (for how to do this, see the 'Launching Print Preview' and 'Using Print Preview' topics earlier). Close the Print Preview window and launch the Database window (see Chapter 3 for how to do this). Then do the following:

Activate one of these tabs

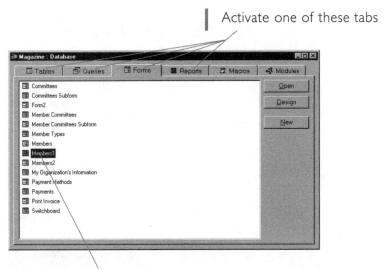

2 Double-click a table, query, form or report

The selected database component is opened. Now pull down the File menu and do the following:

HANDY TIP

If you opened a form or table in step 2 and only want to print specific records, select them *before* you follow step 3.

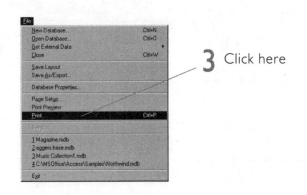

3 Click here

Printing your data (2)

Setting the print criteria
You can:

- specify the printer you want to use

- print the whole database component (the default)

- print a specific page range (e.g. pages 10-15)

- confine the print run to records you selected earlier

- specify the number of copies printed

- turn collation off or on (collation is the process whereby Access prints one full copy at a time. For instance, if you're printing 5 copies of a 12-page database, when collation is active Access prints pages 1-12 of the first copy, 1-12 of the second copy, and so on...)

Carry out any of steps 1-5 below. Finally, follow step 6:

1 Click here; select a printer in the list

If you need to adjust your printer settings, click here: (see your printer's manual for how to do this) before carrying out step 6.

2 Type in the no. of copies

3 Click here to deselect collation

6 Click here to start printing

5 Click here to print selected records only

4 Type in start and end page nos.

Index

N

O

P

Q

R